Dinner Is Ready When You Are

—and a hot, hearty breakfast, too—when you cook the slow, nutritious, old-fashioned way with a modern, electric crock cooker.

In addition to succulent, surefire recipes, *Crockery Cooking* gives you a host of timely tips about caring for your cooker, cooking your food the right amount of time for perfect meals, adapting your own favorite recipes, cooking frozen foods, and freezing leftovers. You can use your cooker to make hot punch, to warm breakfast or dinner rolls, and to keep foods crisp. You'll find time-saving tips about preparing each dish, seasoning with garlic the easy way, dredging meat with flour, and cooking a roast to perfection.

Crockery Cooking is guaranteed to make you a better, more imaginative, more relaxed cook every day of your meal-preparing life.

CROCKERY COOKING
was originally published by
Hopkinson and Blake, Publishers, Inc.

CROCKERY COOKING

A crockful of recipes for electric slow cooking

by PAULA FRANKLIN

(Original title: *The Unwatched Pot*)

Consultant: Rochelle Narotsky, Home Economist, Hamilton Beach

PUBLISHED BY POCKET BOOKS NEW YORK

CROCKERY COOKING

Hopkinson and Blake edition published 1975

POCKET BOOK edition published August, 1975

Standard Book Number: 671-80222-4.
Library of Congress Catalog Card Number: 75-7999.
This POCKET BOOK edition is published by arrangement
with Hopkinson and Blake, Publishers, Inc. Copyright, ©,
1975, by Paula Franklin. All rights reserved. *Crockery Cook-
ing* was originally published under the title *The Unwatched
Pot.* This book, or portions thereof, may not be reproduced
by any means without permission of the original publisher:
Hopkinson and Blake, Publishers, Inc., 329 Fifth Avenue,
New York, N.Y. 10016.
Front cover photograph by Mort Engel.

Printed in the U.S.A.

Contents

CROCKERY COOKING

Slow Cooking

A BIT OF HISTORY

Slow cooking—simmering at low heat for a long time—is probably the second oldest form of cooking invented by the human race. (The oldest is undoubtedly simple roasting over an open fire, with variations such as baking tubers in their own skins in the coals.) Archaeologists digging near the hearths of dwellings in the Ukraine have found cylindrical pits that may date back to 25,000 B.C. Evidence suggests that cooks of the time heated pebbles or stones, lined a pit with them, and then added whatever was on the menu—fish or meats wrapped in leaves were staples in this kind of cooking. They then covered the pit and left it for several hours until the food was done.

This method of slow cookery was still in use thousands of years later among the Indians of North America, who taught early English settlers how to make a proper clambake. The Indian system involved lining a pit with stones and then building a fire on top of them. When the stones were white hot, in went layers of seaweed, clams, and corn, after which the pit was covered and kept moist until clams and corn were tender.

During the centuries between these widely spaced cookouts, dining of course had grown complex and sophisticated. Certain images come to mind: Belshazzar's feast, the symposium of Socrates and his friends, the inspired gluttony of the Romans, medieval banquets enlivened by troubadours, Henry VIII casting half-gnawed bones to his dogs, the triumph of French cuisine under the great chefs of the royal family. Meanwhile, the food of simpler people kept the workaday world going. And it was this type of cooking, rather than the exotic concoctions gracing aristocratic tables, that relied heavily on slow simmering. The medieval cook, whose raw materials were limited, especially in winter, kept a stockpot going most of the time on or near the fire, to be replenished whenever necessary with vegetables, grain, or bits of salt meat. (It would be cleaned out once a year for the meatless meals of Lent.) A vast range of soups, stews and ragouts developed, especially in northern Europe where plentiful forests enabled households to keep a fire going almost continuously.

Not all these one-pot meals sound appealing to us today. A thirteenth-century Persian cookbook gives a recipe for a stew including meat, chickpeas, herbs, cinnamon and rosewater. More bizarre is an English dish composed of, among other things, pickled pork, wine, ale, almonds, cloves, saffron, ginger and pine cones. By the eighteenth century, though, cooks were producing recognizable versions of French cassoulet and pot au feu, Hungarian goulash, Russian borscht, Polish bigos, and German cabbage soup. It was long, slow cooking that made these dishes special—and that makes them appreciated as much today as they were centuries ago.

Electric Slow Cooking

AN INTRODUCTION

The electric slow cooker is a new means of preparing food in a very old way. You can now have all the advantages of this excellent method of cooking without the disadvantages that cooks had to put up with for centuries. Today's technology realizes that no one's in the kitchen with Dinah. Dinah herself isn't there. And you don't have to be either!

Freedom

One of the best features of your electric slow cooker is that it gives you freedom. No longer do you have to hover over a pot to see that food isn't burning. No longer do you have to be on hand all the time to test for doneness. Combine the ingredients as specified, set the dial to the desired temperature, and the cooking will take care of itself. You don't have to be there. Leave your cooker on for hours—or all day, or even all night—without worrying.

This is a new idea for a lot of people, who are used to the cooking process as one requiring constant attention. (And a meal *can* be as demanding as a cranky toddler.) If the notion makes you nervous, try your first two or three recipes while you're at home. You'll soon realize that an electric slow cooker can truly be an unwatched pot.

Low and Slow

Modern stoves are handsome and helpful, but they aren't always ideal for slow cooking. (And, to be realistic, not all of us *have* a modern stove.) If you try to simmer something on a top burner, chances are you'll be constantly adjusting. When the pot boils, you turn it down. The next thing you know, nothing is happening at all. If you do slow cooking in an oven, you may be bothered by varying temperatures. Even when you arrive at a correct one, you can't avoid the fact that cooking for long periods of time heats up your kitchen. The electric slow cooker does away with all these problems.

With a slow cooker you can, in fact, achieve what food experts have described in rather lyrical terms—a true simmer. James Beard calls it "the feeblest ebullition," while *Larousse Gastronomique* defines it as "a slight quivering." According to another writer: "There should be movement, but no violent activity on the surface, nothing more than an occasional gentle plop or the sighing break of a bubble." Now you can create poetry in your kitchen!

Economy

Slow cooking is economical cooking. You can use cheaper cuts of meat. Long simmering makes them tender. And you get more for your money because, with low temperatures, there is less shrinkage. You can also utilize such protein-rich foods as lentils and soybeans, which require long cooking. And, while few red-blooded Americans will spurn fresh corn on the cob that's barely whisked through boiling water, there's much to be said for good, solid, stick-to-the-ribs vegetables like cabbage, potatoes and beans.

Energy Saving

Electric slow cooking saves energy. In these days when Americans are more and more conscious of conserving energy, buying and using yet another electrical appliance may at first sound wasteful. Actually, a slow cooker uses a lot less energy than a major appliance like a range. The low wattage of electric slow cookers makes them modest consumers of electricity. Based on a rate of four cents per kilowatt hour, your cooker will operate all day for a few cents.

Flavor and Nutrition

You will find that food prepared in your electric slow cooker is exceptionally tasty. One reason for this is that heat distribution is even. Another is that liquids are conserved. Meats don't dry out, and other foods, too, keep the tasty juices that make for good eating.

Because foods prepared in an electric slow cooker retain their juices, they also keep more of the nutritive values. Research shows that most nutrients lost in the cooking process pass into the liquid. The more this evaporates—as it does in high-temperature cooking—the less nutritious the food. Other studies indicate that high cooking may actually rob meat protein of some of its amino acids, and can destroy B vitamins. Another health factor: If you use inexpensive meats with little marbling, you will also be cutting down on cholesterol.

Convenience

Your electric slow cooker has additional advantages. (1) One-pot cooking eliminates the need for a multitude of mixing bowls, saucepans and skillets. (2) When foods are cooked at low temperatures, they rarely stick, especially if you have a cooker with the heating unit wrapped around the sides. (3) A slow cooker is useful as a supplementary appliance. You may want to roast a chicken at one temperature and bake some pears at a different setting. No problem. Either item can go into the slow cooker while you put the other one in your oven. (4) An electric slow cooker is a handy way to keep food hot. If your meal is done but people aren't ready to eat, don't worry. Keep the temperature set at low, and another hour or so won't matter. This feature is especially helpful when you're entertaining. (5) An electric slow cooker is portable and inexpensive, so it makes a useful addition for minimally equipped summer cottages and other vacation homes.

The Joy of
an Unwatched Pot

If you've ever been tied down to your kitchen while simmering a soup, braising a beef roast, or poaching a pudding, you'll appreciate the liberated feeling you can get from putting something on to cook and leaving it alone. Great idea, isn't it? Give it a try.

Busy-Day Bonuses

Do you leave your house or apartment in the morning and return late in the afternoon? (Would you like to?) Maybe you're a nine-to-fiver, with a demanding office or factory job. Or you may escape now and then for a day's shopping, a luncheon or a movie. Maybe it's volunteer work that takes up your time, or just a round of errands. With an electric slow cooker, you don't need to rely on chops (expensive) or TV dinners (yeccch) when you get home. Try one of these for a satisfying evening meal:

oxtail and barley soup
basic pot roast
veal and peppers
lima-ham dinner

Company Coming

Entertaining is fun, but not when you have to spend all day getting ready. And who wants to keep dashing out to the kitchen when the living-room conversation is hitting its full stride? Any of these main dishes will bring compliments from your guests, and give you the time to enjoy them:

beef en daube
veal roast with rosemary
chicken tetrazzini
duck Calcutta

If you supplement these with quick-cooking side dishes—rice, noodles or tiny new potatoes—and a good dessert, your party is made.

With a Foreign Flavor

In the last few years Americans have learned to like, and prepare, a variety of foods from all over the world. And a great many national cuisines feature dishes that especially lend themselves to long, slow cooking. Here are just a few from the many this book contains:

borscht
osso buco
bigos
sweet and sour pork
arroz con pollo

Quickies but Goodies

In terms of slow cooking, a "quicky" will take a mere three hours to prepare, instead of the more usual eight or ten. Lest that sound frightening, remember that there are many occasions when you plan to be gone for just about that amount of time —attending a meeting, taking in a play or going to

16   Crockery Cooking / *The Joy of an Unwatched Pot*

a football game. When you come home, you can plan on bringing friends with you to enjoy one of the following:

Swedish meat balls
barbecued spoonburgers
seafood Naples
kidney beans with cheese

Fix a bowl of crisp raw vegetables before you go, have some good bread or rolls on hand, and, if you own one, prepare your automatic coffee pot so it's ready to go. In a matter of minutes, your meal will be on the table.

Is There a Man in the Kitchen?

It goes without saying (or should) that any of the recipes in this book can be prepared by anybody, regardless of sex or previous condition of servitude. It's true, however, that, except for European chefs in their lofty white hats, men have usually stayed out of the kitchen in droves. Habits are changing in this respect, which is all to the good. Still, a lot of men are novices at cooking, so here are some ridiculously simple recipes you can start with:

Swiss steak
lamb stroganoff
scalloped ham and potatoes
sherry-olive chicken

Food to Spare

Many of the recipes included here produce four, six, eight or more servings. If you're cooking for two, don't despair. Aside from asking friends or relatives in to share your meal, you can cook ahead and save yourself some time. Most people don't mind leftovers if they have a breather in between. If you've had lamb stew on Monday, try macaroni and cheese on Tuesday before breaking out the stew again. Speaking of stew, you can throw in another vegetable or two to vary things the second time around.

Another possibility, of course, is the freezer. Even if you have just a small space for freezing, it will usually hold a plastic container that will give you a ready-cooked meal in no time. Here are just a few of the foods that freeze well:

pot roast
stuffed peppers
chili con carne
spaghetti sauce
roast chicken

Be sure the container is closed tightly. If the lid is loose, seal it with a strip of tape. Don't forget to add a label describing the contents and giving the date you froze them.

You can heat frozen foods in your slow cooker if you wish—either dishes you've frozen yourself, or packaged foods you've bought. Use a low or automatic setting and, if you're heating store-bought goods, follow the package directions for adding water, etc. (using somewhat less liquid than called for). Time depends on the size and contents of the package; 3-4 hours on the automatic setting will be good for most frozen vegetables. Keep this elementary precaution in mind: Don't place ice-cold food directly in contact with a *hot* cooker. If the liner is made of crockery or glass, it may crack.

General Use and Care

There are many different models of electric slow cookers. See the next section—"Pots for Slow Cooking"—for information on specific appliances. The following are general tips only.

Before using your own cooker, read carefully the directions for use and maintenance that come with it.

General Safety

1. Keep your cooker out of reach of small children or inquisitive animals.

2. Unplug your slow cooker after using it.

3. If you drop or otherwise damage your cooker, or if it doesn't work correctly, don't try to use it. Return it to your nearest authorized facility for examination, repair or adjustment.

4. Your appliance has a short cord to minimize danger from tripping or becoming entangled. You may use an extension cord if it has a marked electrical rating at least as great as the electrical rating of the cooker.

Timing

The recipes in this book specify a certain number of hours according to low, high or automatic settings. The low setting, which uses 70 to 80 watts in most slow cookers, produces a temperature in the range of 170° to 200°. The high setting, which uses 140 to 160 watts in most slow cookers, will produce temperatures up to 280°. The automatic setting is a thermostat cycling setting, which alternates between the 70-80 watt low heating elements and the 140-160 watt high heating elements; it produces a temperature of 200°. The time a cooker takes to reach the temperatures of 170°-200° (low), 280° (high), and 200° (automatic) will vary depending on the volume of the food and its initial temperature. Cool or cold food will extend the cooking time, and warm food will shorten it.

Final cooking temperatures are determined by liquid content and density of the food mass. Consult the directions for your cooker and make the necessary timing adjustments.

Remember that the times suggested here are approximate. If food doesn't get done in the amount of time specified in a recipe, one of these factors may be to blame:

• Voltage variations. In some areas, because of energy conservation or high power consumption, the voltage is lower than the normal 110/120. Longer cooking time is thus necessary.

• Temperature variations. Cold or frozen foods will take longer to cook than those at room temperature.

• Altitude. At high altitudes (over 4,000 feet), food takes longer to cook.

Be sure to allow ample time for cooking. It is practically impossible to overcook food in an electric slow cooker. Slow cooking is gentle cooking, and an extra hour or two—especially when the dial is set on low or automatic—will do no harm.

If you do want to limit cooking time when you're not around to make adjustments, there are two ways of doing so: (1) You can buy an electric timer. Set it to turn your cooker on at the time you wish. (2) If you have an electric stove, it may have a timing device and an outlet. Plug in your cooker and set the timer to turn it on (not off).

Keep this rule of thumb in mind: One hour of cooking on the high setting is equal to about 2½ hours on low. Also, any recipe recommending an automatic setting can be used with a non-automatic model. Simply start to cook on high for about 2 hours and then switch to low; extend the overall cooking time slightly.

Some Things You Should Know

• All the recipes in this book are to be cooked with the lid on. *Leave it on.* If it's glass, you can check on your food without opening the pot. In any case, you lose steam and the water seal around the lid—which prolongs the cooking period—every time you peek inside. Just be patient.

• Stirring is not usually required. However, if the dial is set on high and you're home, an occasional stir won't hurt.

• Your slow cooker should be at least half filled for best results. If you're cooking less, cover the food with aluminum foil.

• When cooking vegetables and meats together on the low setting, put the vegetables in the pot first.

This will raise up the meat to permit proper liquid circulation; also the vegetables will stay moister that way. When adding liquids, do so last.

• You may occasionally end up with too much liquid, since the moisture content of foods varies. The excess can be reduced if you remove the cover of your cooker and set the dial on high until the excess liquid evaporates.

• You may want to try using a trivet or meat rack in the bottom of your cooker. It's useful for keeping rather fatty meats, such as pork or duck, out of their cooking juices (which, naturally, tend to be fatty, too).

• You can make gravy in several different ways. (1) Add minute tapioca to the recipe while cooking. (2) Remove foods from pot; take out 1-2 tablespoons of juice, blend with flour or cornstarch, and return to the pot, cooking about 15 minutes on high. (3) Remove the juices to a saucepan and make the gravy there.

• You don't have to thaw frozen foods before putting them into your cooker if (a) the cooker isn't hot to begin with; or (b) you add the food to something that's cooking, mixing it in so that the frozen food isn't in direct contact with the hot cooker. However, many recipes in this book do suggest adding thawed frozen vegetables in the last hour or so of cooking. This avoids any danger of cracking glass or crockery liners. It saves time, too.

• If you have trouble with certain foods taking a long time to get done (whether or not you live in a low-voltage area), here are some suggestions: (1) With dried beans, use precooked or canned ones rather than beans soaked overnight. (2) In the case of dense vegetables (cauliflower, celery, broccoli or cabbage), slice or quarter them; or you might prefer to steam or parboil them before adding them to the cooker. (3) Root vegetables such as carrots and turnips will cook faster if they are diced. (4) Large pieces of meat (2-4 pounds) may be cut into smaller chunks.

Adapting Recipes

An electric slow cooker can be used for a wide variety of soups, sauces, casseroles, stews and braised meats and vegetables, as well as for baked fruits and breads. If you have a favorite recipe that isn't included here, or want to try something new in your electric cooker, the following suggestions should be helpful:

• To judge *cooking time,* use a similar recipe in this book. Most meat and vegetable combinations require seven hours or more on low.

• *Meats* do not always need to be browned, though you may want to do so in order to remove excess fat —from bacon, ground beef or duck, for example.

• *Vegetables* do not need to be sautéed in advance, except in a few cases (for instance, onions for onion soup). One exception is eggplant, which has a strong flavor and should be parboiled or sautéed before being combined with other foods.

• *Herbs and spices* may behave differently in an electric slow cooker. Whole herbs and spices may give more flavor than usual, ground ones less. Season carefully, taste before serving, and correct seasonings then if necessary.

• *Milk, cream and sour cream* may curdle if left in a cooker for many hours. It is best to add them in the last hour of cooking. If a recipe specifies one of these ingredients as the only liquid in the cooking process, you may substitute evaporated milk, water or condensed soup, such as cream of mushroom or chicken.

• *Pasta and rice* may disintegrate after long hours in a slow cooker. Add them in the last hour of cooking.

• *Liquid* is well conserved in an electric slow cooker. Vegetables such as onions and tomatoes give off additional liquid. Therefore, in adapting most recipes, try using less than specified—in any case, no more than enough to cover the food. Note, however, that more liquid will evaporate on the high setting than on the low.

Pots for Slow Cooking

Electric slow cookers are made in a wide range of styles. The one characteristic they share is that all of them make use of electric heating coils plus a container for food. The cooker may consist of a single unit, in which case it is usually not immersible in water. (The exception: pots with removable temperature-control units.) Or the container may rest on or in a separate heating unit. Such a container (but *not* the heating unit) can be washed like an ordinary casserole, in the sink or in the dishwasher.

Most single-unit pots are made with the coils wrapped around the liner, which promotes even heat distribution. Usually those with separate containers are heated only from below, and some sticking may result.

Cooker capacities vary from two to eight quarts. The container may be made of crockery (that is, earthenware), glass, or metal. Metal liners often have a coating of Teflon or similar material.

The temperature dial may be attached to the pot or detachable. It may have low and high settings, numbered settings, or actual temperature indicators, like an oven. An automatic setting, a feature of several cookers, starts at high, switches to low, and then shifts back and forth between the two. Cooked at this setting, food takes less time than it would on low, more than on high. Some cookers have a wide range of temperature settings, and can be used for browning or sautéing.

Consider your own needs before you buy. If you're cooking for a crowd, get one of the larger pots. (But remember that even a "standard" 3- or 3½-quart size can easily hold dinner for six.) If you can't bear to wash pots by hand, you'll want to investigate the cookers with containers that separate from their heating units.

Again we stress the point that before you use your own cooker, you should read carefully the directions for use and maintenance you'll find with it.

Note: Appliances described in this section are listed alphabetically according to manufacturer. Product names and trademarks are registered.

- **CORNING**
  Table Range, Table Range Plus
  Basic features: Corning ware skillet rests on separate heating base. Glass lid. Detachable cord.
  Size: 10-inch skillet
            (*Table Range Plus* also has 5-quart saucepan.)
  Temperature information: Dial has settings from 200° F. to 500° F. Set dial at 240° F. when recipe calls for low, at 350° F. when it calls for high.

- **CORNWALL**

  ### Crockery Cooker (1-piece)

  Basic features: Single-unit pot with painted metal exterior. Glass lid.

  Sizes: #2843: 4 quarts, glass liner

  #2844: 4 quarts, crockery liner

  #2866: 6 quarts, crockery liner

  Temperature information: Dial has medium and high settings. (Use medium setting when recipe calls for low.) Models #2843 and #2866 also have automatic shift, which starts pot on high, then shifts to low.

  ### Crockery Cooker (2-piece)

  Basic features: Crockery pot rests on separate heating base. Glass lid.

  Sizes: 3 quarts

  4½ quarts

  Temperature information: Dial has medium and high settings. (Use medium setting when recipe calls for low.)

- **DOMINION**

  ### Crock-a-Dial

  Basic features: Single-unit crockery pot with painted metal exterior. Glass lid.

  Size: 4 quarts

  Temperature information: Dial has low and high settings, plus automatic shift, which starts pot on high, then shifts to low.

  ### Crock-a-Dial II

  Basic features: Single-unit glass pot with painted metal exterior. Glass lid.

  Size: 4 quarts

  Temperature information: Dial has low and high settings. Automatic shift available on one model.

- **FARBERWARE**
  Pot-Pourri
  Basic features: Single-unit stainless-steel pot and lid. Detachable cord with temperature-control unit.

  Size: 5 quarts

  Temperature information: Dial has settings from 100° F. to 500° F. (Settings above 300° F. are used for regular cooking or deep-fat frying.) Set dial at 200° F. when recipe calls for low, at 250° F. when it calls for high. Since these cookers heat up quickly, shorten recipe cooking times by a third to a half.

- **GRANDINETTI**
  All-American Crockery Cook Pot
  Basic features: Single-unit crockery pot with painted metal exterior. Glass lid on 3½-quart size, plastic lid on 5-quart size. Detachable cord with temperature-control unit on larger size only.

  Sizes: 3½ quarts
          5 quarts

  Temperature information: Dial has low and high settings.

- **HAMILTON BEACH**
  Continental Cooker, Crock Watcher,
  Simmer-On
  Basic features: Single-unit pot with painted metal exterior. *Continental Cooker* has glass liner; others have crockery liners. Glass lids.

  Size: 4 quarts

  Temperature information: Dial has low and high settings. *Continental Cooker* and *Crock Watcher* also have automatic shift, which starts pot on high, then shifts to low.

- **NESCO**
  Potluck
  Basic features: Oval metal liner fits into separate metal pot with painted exterior. Detachable cord. Available with either glass or metal lid.

  Size: 6 quarts

  Temperature information: Dial has settings from 200° F. to 500° F. (Settings above 300° F. are used for roasting.) Set dial at 200° F. when recipe calls for low, at 250° F. when it calls for high. Since this cooker heats up quickly, shorten recipe cooking times by a third to a half.

- **OSTER**
  Super Pot Slow-Fast Cooker
  Basic features: Single-unit porcelainized aluminum pot and lid. Interior lined with Teflon-type cooking surface.

  Sizes: 5 quarts
  8 quarts

  Temperature information: Dial has settings from 200° F. to 450° F. (Settings above 300° F. are used for regular cooking or deep-fat frying.) Set dial at 200° F. when recipe calls for low, at 300° F. when it calls for high. Since this cooker heats up quickly, shorten recipe cooking times by a third to a half.

- **J. C. PENNEY**
  Slow Cooker/Fryer
  Basic Features: Crockery pot fits into separate metal fryer unit. Metal lid.

  Size: 3-quart cooker fits into 5-quart fryer.

  Temperature information: Dial has settings from "simmer" (about 200° F.) to 400° F. (Higher settings are used for deep-fat frying.) Set dial at simmer when recipe calls for low, between 325° F., and 350° F. when it calls for high.

Slow Crockery Cooker

Basic features: Single-unit crockery pot with painted metal exterior. Glass lid.

Size: 3½ quarts

Temperature information: Dial has low and high settings.

• PRESTO
Presto Slow Cooker

Basic features: Single-unit cast-aluminum pot lined with Teflon-type cooking surface. Glass lid. Detachable cord with temperature-control unit.

Sizes: 2¾ quarts
       5 quarts

Temperature information: Dial has low, high, and "brown" settings. Since these cookers heat up quickly, shorten recipe cooking times by a third to a half.

• RIVAL
Casserole Crock Pot

Basic features: Crockery pot fits into separate metal container. Plastic lid.

Size: 3 quarts

Temperature information: Dial has low and high settings.

Crock Pot

Basic features: Single-unit crockery pot with painted metal exterior. Glass lids on 2- and 3½-quart sizes. Others have plastic lids; these models also have detachable cords with temperature-control units.

Sizes: 2 quarts
3 quarts
3½ quarts
5 quarts

Temperature information: Dial has low and high settings.

- ## SEARS (SIMPSONS)
  ### Crockery Cooker (1-piece)
  Basic features: Single-unit crockery pot with painted metal exterior. Glass lid.

  Size: 4 quarts

  Temperature information: Dial has medium and high settings. (Use medium setting when recipe calls for low.)

  ### Crockery Cooker (2-piece)
  Basic features: Crockery pot rests on separate heating base. Glass lid.

  Sizes: 2½ quarts
  5 quarts

  Temperature information: Dial has settings numbered 1, 2, and 3. For 2½-quart size, use setting 3 when recipe calls for low (pot cannot be used for recipes requiring a high setting). For 5-quart size, setting 2 equals low, setting 3 equals high.

- ## SUNBEAM
  ### Crockery Cooker/Fryer
  Basic features: Crockery pot fits into separate metal fryer unit. Metal lid.

  Size: 3-quart cooker fits into 5-quart fryer.

  Temperature information: Dial has settings from simmer (about 200° F.) to 400° F. (Higher settings are used for deep-fat frying.) Set dial at simmer when recipe calls for low, between 325° F. and 350° F. when it calls for high.

- **WARDS (VAN WYCK)**
  Sim-R-Pot
  Basic features: Single-unit glass pot with painted metal exterior. Glass lid. Detachable cord.
  Size: 3½ quarts
  Temperature information: Dial has low and and high settings. Use high setting when recipe calls for low. Appliance does not reach higher temperatures, although recipes requiring them may get done if cooked for several hours longer than specified.

- **WEST BEND**
  Colonial Cooker, Home Maid,
  Lazy Day Slo-Cooker
  Basic features: Metal liner fits into separate metal pot. *Home Maid* has glass lid; others have metal lids. *Lazy Day* has detachable cord.
  Sizes: 4 quarts (*Home Maid*)
         5 quarts (*Colonial Cooker*)
         6 quarts (*Lazy Day*)
  Temperature information: Dial has settings numbered from 1 to 5. Use setting 2 when recipe calls for low, setting 4 when it calls for high.
  Colonial Crock
  Basic features: Crockery liner fits into separate crockery pot.
  Size: 2 quarts
  Temperature information: Dial has settings numbered from 1 to 4. Use setting 2 when recipe calls for low, setting 4 when it calls for high.

About This Book

There are infinite ways of writing about food. This book attempts to keep recipes simple and to describe the steps in their preparation clearly. A few words of additional explanation may be helpful.

- In most cases, ingredients are listed in the order in which they should be placed in the cooker, or in which they are to be prepared. However, most meat dishes list the meat first, as it is the basic ingredient.
- Potatoes, carrots and onions are to be peeled unless the recipe states otherwise.
- The terms "broth" and "stock" are used interchangeably, although the former usually indicates a canned product. You can make either beef or chicken stock by dissolving a bouillon cube in boiling water.
- In most cases, the general term "shortening" has been preferred to a more specific listing of butter, margarine, vegetable oil, bacon grease or lard. Let your personal preference be your guide.
- Herbs are dried unless otherwise specified. If you can obtain fresh ones, by all means use them. Multiply the dried quantity by two or three when using fresh herbs. A bouquet garni is a collection of

herbs—if dried, wrapped in a cheesecloth bundle; if fresh, tied with a string.

- Mushrooms and parsley are fresh unless otherwise specified.

- Most canned goods are listed according to their weight—that is, by ounces or pounds—rather than by can number. An exception is soup, since most soup cans contain roughly the same amount (around 10-11 ounces).

- Canned soups are not to be diluted unless so specified.

- Amounts are given for salt and pepper. As with all seasonings, however, these are approximate. You should taste, test and correct to get the flavor you like. White pepper has not been specified, by the way. Consider using it with any dish that is light in color, such as a chowder or a fish dish.

- A handy way to dredge meat—that is, coat it with flour (usually seasoned)—is to mix the flour, salt and pepper in a paper or plastic bag. Then add some or all of the meat, depending on quantities, and shake.

- Substitutions can be made in many cases. If you can get *good* fresh tomatoes (not the plastic kind), they're certainly preferable to canned ones. (But you'll have to peel them.) If you can't get leeks, use mild onions instead. If you prefer organic ingredients, such as sea salt, honey or natural sugar, by all means use them.

Remember: a cookbook is a guide, not a straitjacket!

Beginning the Day

In these times when everyone is in a hurry, breakfast especially gets short-changed. But there's something satisfying about a hot meal at the beginning of the day, particularly on a cold winter morning or when you have many hours of hard work ahead of you. If you're "of a certain age," as the French say, you may remember your mother putting cereal on to cook at night at the back of the range. An electric slow cooker makes the task much easier.

BREAKFAST OATMEAL

2 cups old-fashioned 1 teaspoon salt
 rolled oats   ½ cup chopped dates
4 cups water

1. Combine all ingredients in cooker.
2. Cook on low 8 hours (overnight).

Yield: 6 servings

CREAM OF WHEAT

⅔ cup cream of wheat ½ teaspoon salt
3¾ cups water

1. Combine all ingredients in cooker.
2. Cook on low 8 hours (overnight).
3. Serve with brown sugar or maple syrup.

Yield: 4 servings

Note: You may want to cook the cereal with ½ cup raisins for extra flavor.

GRITS

Northerners having their first restaurant breakfast in the South are often surprised at the bonus they get with their eggs and bacon. If it looks like cereal, it's probably grits—coarsely ground hominy (hulled corn). Anyway, it's good up North, too.

⅔ cup grits   ¾ teaspoon salt
3½ cups water

1. Combine all ingredients in cooker.
2. Cook on low 8 hours (overnight).

Yield: 4 servings

FRIED CORNMEAL MUSH

This is delicious served with syrup or jam. It also goes well with main-course dishes, especially those made with pork or ham.

½ cup yellow cornmeal   flour
½ teaspoon salt   butter or margarine
2 cups boiling water

1. Combine first three ingredients in cooker.
2. Cook on high 1 hour.
3. Pour cooked mush into a container—a 17-ounce fruit can is just right—and chill thoroughly.
4. Unmold mush. Cut into slices about ⅜ inch thick.
5. Dip slices in flour and sauté in butter or margarine.

Yield: 4 servings

HINTS FOR THE COOK

• If you have some baked breakfast rolls on hand
—Danish pastries, doughnuts, pecan rolls, or the like
—and want to warm them up, use your slow cooker.
Start with the rolls at room temperature. Simply turn
the cooker to low, place the rolls inside, cover them,
and heat for about half an hour.

• A slow cooker is a handy place to store cookies
or rolls when it's not in use. Keep it in mind, too, for
opened bags of potato chips or pretzels.

Soups

Short cuts for producing soup are abundant—condensed soup in cans, dehydrated soup in foil packages, powdered soup in boxes. Some of them taste surprisingly good. But none can really compare with the home-made variety, whether it's a restorative chicken soup (universally recommended for low spirits), a rich black bean concoction, a bowl of minestrone, or a hearty vegetable-beef combination. Another advantage of making your own soup is that it inspires improvisation. With many of these recipes, and other favorites of your own, you can feel free to add leftover pasta, meat, or vegetables that have been cluttering up your refrigerator.

HAM-BROCCOLI CHOWDER

2 tablespoons flour
1 small can evaporated milk
2 cups diced ham
1 package frozen chopped broccoli

¼ cup minced onion
1 cup grated Swiss cheese
2 cups water
1 cup light cream

1. Mix flour and milk in cooker.
2. Add other ingredients except cream.
3. Cook on low 7 hours, or on automatic 4 hours.
4. Before serving, stir in cream and heat.

Yield: 6 servings

LEEK AND ASPARAGUS CHOWDER

3 tablespoons flour
½ cup water
1 10-ounce package
  frozen cut asparagus,
  thawed
1 12-ounce can white
  whole-kernel corn
3 cups sliced mush-
  rooms
3 large leeks, sliced

1 tablespoon minced
  pimiento
½ teaspoon salt
¼ teaspoon white
  pepper
4 tablespoons butter
2 cups chicken broth
1 13-ounce can evapo-
  rated milk

1 cup light cream

1. Combine flour and water in cooker.
2. Add all other ingredients except cream to cooker.
3. Cook on automatic 4 hours.
4. Before serving, stir in cream and heat.

Yield: 6-8 servings

FISH CHOWDER

Our word "chowder" comes from the French *chaudière,* a covered pot or kettle. The term now usually means a soup that includes milk. Note that if you are going to simmer any chowder in a slow cooker for more than 4 hours, evaporated milk is better than fresh milk.

1 cup chopped onion	1 13-ounce can evaporated milk
½ cup butter or margarine	½ cup water
½ cup diced salt pork	2 cups flaked cooked fish (red snapper, haddock or perch)
3 medium potatoes, diced	

1 cup cream

1. Sauté onion and salt pork in butter until soft.
2. Flake cooked fish, removing bones and skin.
3. Combine all ingredients except cream in cooker.
4. Cook on high 2 hours, then switch to low 4-6 hours. Or cook on automatic 5-6 hours.
5. Before serving, stir in cream and heat.

Yield: 6 servings

POTATO CHOWDER

6 slices bacon, diced
3 tablespoons chopped
   onion
5 medium potatoes,
   diced

1 cup chopped carrots
1 teaspoon salt
1 package frozen
   chopped spinach

1½ cups milk

1. Fry bacon bits until crisp; discard fat.
2. Combine all ingredients except milk in cooker.
   Add water to cover.
3. Cook on high 2 hours, then switch to low 4 hours.
   Or cook on automatic for 5 hours.
4. Before serving, stir in milk and heat.

Yield: 6 servings

VICHYSSOISE

Please pronounce the final "s." It's "vee shee swahz," no matter what kind of stares you get from the waiter or the clods at the next table. And it was invented at the Ritz Carlton Hotel in New York City, by the way.

5 medium potatoes, sliced	1½ tablespoons salt
4 leeks (white and lightest green parts), sliced	2 cups chicken stock
	2 cups milk
	1 cup heavy cream
1 large onion, chopped	chopped fresh or frozen chives

1. Combine all ingredients except last three in cooker. Cook on high 3 hours.
2. Purée mixture in blender or food mill and return to cooker.
3. Add milk and cream, stir well, and heat to boiling —about 1 hour on high.
4. Chill.
5. Serve with chives.

Yield: 6-8 servings

Note: If chilled soup is too thick for your taste, add additional milk or cream.

CREAM OF BARLEY SOUP

Barley was a staple of the diet of the early Greeks, who ate barley paste, barley gruel and barley bread. Hippocrates prescribed barley water for a multitude of complaints. This rich soup has a pleasantly smoky flavor, and is a good prelude to a meal featuring broiled meat or chicken.

⅓ cup pearl barley
½ cup chopped onion
½ cup chopped celery
½ cup chopped leeks (optional)
1 small smoked ham hock
4 cups chicken stock

* bouquet garni consisting of 4 sprigs parsley, ¼ teaspoon thyme, and 1 small bay leaf

2 tablespoons instant mashed potatoes
½ cup heavy cream

1. Combine all ingredients except mashed potatoes and cream in cooker.
2. Cook on low 4-5 hours.
3. Remove ham hock and discard (or use it to flavor another soup). Also discard bouquet garni.
4. Add instant mashed potatoes and cream; cook on high for 15 minutes.

Yield: 6 servings

* See pages 33–34.

BORSCHT

This famous soup, known throughout the Slavic countries, has endless variations. The only ingredient all versions have in common is beets. It is just about impossible to overcook borscht, especially if you add one or more beets at the end to supply the characteristic red color.

2 stalks celery, diced	4 sprigs parsley
2 carrots, chopped	1 bay leaf
2 leeks, sliced	1 teaspoon salt
1 white turnip, diced	1 teaspoon sugar
½ small cabbage, cut into chunks	1 1-pound can tomatoes, with juice
3 beets, diced	
1 large onion, chopped	1 beet
1 clove garlic, crushed	1 cup beef stock
1½ pounds stewing beef, cut into 1-inch pieces	1 tablespoon wine vinegar
	sour cream

1. Combine all ingredients except last four in cooker.
2. Cook on high 2 hours, then switch to low 9 hours. Or cook on automatic 10 hours.
3. Grate 1 beet or cut in julienne strips. Simmer in 1 cup beef stock and 1 tablespoon vinegar for 2-3 minutes. Add to soup.
4. Serve borscht with generous dollops of sour cream.

Yield: 6 servings

CABBAGE SOUP

2 slices bacon, diced
½ small cabbage, cut in chunks
2 carrots, sliced
2 white turnips, diced
2 leeks, sliced
2 medium potatoes, diced

1 tablespoon chopped chives
1 tablespoon chopped parsley
1½ teaspoons salt
⅛ teaspoon pepper

grated Parmesan cheese

1. Sauté bacon and discard fat.
2. Combine all ingredients except cheese in cooker. Cover with water.
3. Cook on low 12 hours, or on high 8 hours.
4. Serve sprinkled with grated cheese.

Yield: 4-5 servings

ONION SOUP

3 medium onions, sliced very thin
¼ cup butter or margarine
1 teaspoon salt
1 tablespoon sugar

2 tablespoons flour
1 quart beef stock
½ cup dry white wine or dry vermouth

French bread
Parmesan cheese

1. Sauté onions in butter in covered skillet until soft. Uncover, add salt and sugar, and cook 15 minutes. Stir in flour and cook for 3 minutes longer.
2. Combine onions, stock and wine in cooker.
3. Cook on low 6-8 hours.
4. Serve with toasted rounds of French bread topped with cheese. If you have earthenware bowls, fill with soup, top with toasted bread and cheese, and place under preheated broiler for 2-3 minutes. Or you can toast the bread, sprinkle with cheese, broil, and then place on top of soup served in standard soup plates.

Yield: 6-8 servings

BLACK BEAN SOUP

Though this rich soup requires some extra effort, it is worth the time, being practically a meal in itself. Serve with French or sourdough bread, a tray of celery and carrot sticks, and dessert.

1 cup black beans	1 bay leaf
1 stalk celery, chopped	1 teaspoon pepper
1 medium onion, chopped	1 quart water
1 leek, sliced	½ cup sherry or Madeira wine
1 pound smoked pork butt	½ lemon, thinly sliced
¼ cup chopped fresh parsley (or 2 tablespoons dried)	1 hard-boiled egg, grated

1. Wash beans. Soak overnight in water to cover.
2. Combine all ingredients except wine, lemon and egg in cooker.
3. Cook on high 3 hours, then switch to low 9 hours. Or cook on automatic 10 hours.
4. Remove and discard bay leaf. Remove meat and cut into pieces, discarding fat.
5. Purée beans and liquid in blender or food mill and return to cooker, along with meat.
6. Add wine and reheat soup. Serve in individual bowls, float lemon slice on top and sprinkle with egg.

Yield: 6 servings

LENTIL SOUP

According to the Bible, Esau sold his birthright for "a mess of pottage" (French *potage*, meaning "soup"). Students of such things have decided that the medium of exchange may have been lentils.

1½ cups lentils
  2 medium onions, chopped
  3 stalks celery, chopped
  ½ cup parsley, chopped

1 8-ounce can tomato sauce
1 tablespoon salt
½ teaspoon basil

4 tablespoons flour
4 tablespoons butter or margarine

1. Soak lentils in water overnight.
2. Combine all ingredients except flour and butter in cooker. Add water to cover.
3. Cook on low 10-12 hours, or on high 5-6 hours.
4. To thicken soup, remove ¼ cup liquid and combine with flour and butter. Return mixture to cooker.

Yield: 8-10 servings

LIMA BEAN SOUP

1 cup small lima beans
½ cup pearl barley
1 onion, diced
4 carrots, sliced
6 stalks celery, chopped
½ small cabbage, cut in slivers
1 medium potato, diced
½ pound spinach, torn into small pieces
1 small package dried mushrooms
¼ pound butter or margarine
1½ teaspoons salt
¼ teaspoon pepper
2 bouillon cubes

1. Combine all ingredients in cooker.
2. Cook on high 2 hours, then switch to low 6 hours. Or cook on automatic 7 hours.

Yield: 6 servings

NAVY BEAN SOUP

2 cups navy beans
1 cup chopped onion
3 sprigs celery leaves
1 pound ham or smoked
  pork butt

1 bay leaf
1 teaspoon salt
6 whole peppercorns

1. Soak beans in water overnight.
2. Combine all ingredients in cooker. Add water to cover.
3. Cook on low 10-12 hours, or on high 5-6 hours.
4. Remove ham or pork from soup, cut into pieces, and return to pot.

Yield: 8-10 servings

PEA SOUP

2 cups dried split peas
1 cup chopped onions
½ cup sliced celery
1 ham hock or ¼
  pound salt pork

1 bay leaf
1 teaspoon salt
6 whole peppercorns

1. Soak peas in water overnight.
2. Combine all ingredients in cooker. Cover with water.
3. Cook on low 10-12 hours, on high 5-6 hours, or on automatic 7 hours.

Yield: 6 servings

Note: Soup may be thinned with hot milk if it seems too thick.

MINESTRONE

This thick Italian soup may be made with various ingredients, but it always includes chickpeas (also known as garbanzos). A heavy sprinkling of cheese is also a must.

¼ pound ham, minced
1 1-pound can chickpeas
½ cup minced onion
1 clove garlic, minced
½ cup diced carrots
½ cup diced celery
1 cup fresh spinach, chopped

1 fresh tomato, diced (or 1 10-ounce can, drained)
1 medium potato, diced
½ cup salt pork, diced
2 tablespoons chopped parsley
1 quart chicken broth

½ cup elbow macaroni

grated Parmesan cheese

1. Sauté salt pork and discard fat.
2. Combine all ingredients except macaroni and cheese in cooker. Add water if chicken broth does not cover.
3. Cook on high 1 hour, then switch to low 6-8 hours. Or cook on automatic 5-6 hours.
4. One half hour before serving, add macaroni. Serve soup generously sprinkled with cheese.

Yield: 6 servings

IBERIAN CHICKPEA SOUP

1 20-ounce can chick-
  peas, drained (re-
  serve liquid)
2 onions, chopped
4 cloves garlic, finely
  minced
2 cups diced potatoes
3 cups finely chopped
  cabbage

1 hambone or ham
  hock
1-2 cooked Spanish
  sausages (if not
  available, use
  peperoni)
2 bay leaves
pinch saffron
1½ teaspoons salt
¼ teaspoon pepper

1. Combine all ingredients in cooker.
2. Pour in enough chickpea liquid to cover; if not
   sufficient, add water.
3. Cook on high 2 hours, then on low 5 hours. Or
   cook on automatic 6 hours.

Yield: 8-10 servings

SPANISH SOUP

¼ pound chickpeas
¼ pound white marrow beans
¼ pound salt pork, diced
¼ pound smoked ham, diced
¼ pound Spanish sausage (or any garlic sausage)
4 small potatoes, diced
2 tomatoes, chopped (or 1 1-pound can, drained)

2 cloves garlic, finely minced
1 hambone (optional)
1½ teaspoons ground cumin
1½ teaspoons salt
¼ teaspoon pepper

½ pound chopped spinach

croutons

1. Wash chickpeas and beans. Soak overnight in water to cover.
2. Sauté salt pork, ham and sausage. Discard fat. Cut sausage into thin slices.
3. Combine all ingredients except spinach and croutons in cooker.
4. Cook on low 15 hours, or on automatic 8 hours.
5. Stir in spinach and cook until wilted.
6. Serve with croutons.

Yield: 10-12 servings

WINTER VEGETABLE SOUP

2 cups sliced leeks
3 cups diced potatoes
2 cups sliced carrots
1½ cups diced turnips
3 cups diced yellow
  squash
1 small cauliflower,
  cut into small florets

1 package frozen peas
1½ teaspoons savory
1 bay leaf, crushed
2½ cups chicken stock

grated Parmesan cheese
fresh dill weed, chopped

1. Combine all ingredients except cheese and dill in cooker.
2. Cook on high 5 hours, or on automatic 6 hours.
3. Serve sprinkled with grated cheese and chopped dill.

Yield: 6 servings

HEARTY VEGETABLE SOUP

2 pounds lean stewing beef, cut into 1-inch cubes
2 large potatoes, diced
2 onions, chopped
3 carrots, sliced
2 stalks celery, sliced (include tops for flavor)
6-8 sprigs parsley

1 tablespoon salt
½ teaspoon thyme
¼ teaspoon pepper
1 1-pound can tomatoes (with juice), chopped
1 can water

1 package frozen mixed vegetables, thawed

1. Combine all ingredients except frozen mixed vegetables in cooker.
2. Cook on low 10-11 hours.
3. Add frozen mixed vegetables and heat through.

Yield: 6-8 servings

Note: You may add or substitute other fresh or frozen vegetables, such as cabbage, green or wax beans, or turnips. If they are already cooked, add them in the last hour or so of cooking.

CHICKEN-VEGETABLE SOUP

3 carrots, quartered
3 stalks celery, cut into
1-inch slices
1 medium onion, finely
chopped

2 pounds chicken backs
and wings
1 tablespoon salt
½ teaspoon pepper
2 quarts hot water

1. Combine all ingredients in cooker and stir thoroughly.
2. Cook on low 7 hours, on high 3½ hours, or on automatic 5 hours.
3. Remove chicken pieces from soup. Discard skin and bones and return meat to soup.

Yield: 6 servings

OXTAIL AND BARLEY SOUP

Like most combinations using meat and grain, this is a hearty stick-to-the-ribs dish. Serve it with crisp bread and have plenty of fresh fruit for dessert.

½ cup pearl barley
2 medium onions, sliced very thin
3 celery ribs, chopped (include leafy tops for flavor)
3 carrots, peeled and cut in slices

1 bay leaf
2 teaspoons salt
½ teaspoon pepper
½ teaspoon thyme
2 pounds oxtails, disjointed

chopped fresh parsley

1. Combine all ingredients except parsley in cooker.
2. Cook on low 12 hours.
3. When soup cools, take out bay leaf. Remove oxtails from broth, cut meat from bones, and discard the latter. Return meat to soup. (You can skim fat from soup at this stage or refrigerate overnight and then do so.)
4. Reheat soup and sprinkle with parsley.

Yield: 6 servings

LEEK AND SAUSAGE SOUP

Sausage has a long history, dating back to Babylonian and Egyptian times. Almost every region of the world has its own specialty, depending on local produce and tastes. Most of us are familiar with Italian salami (from the Latin word for "salting"), and bologna (from the town of the same name). It's easy enough to tell where in Germany frankfurters originated. Would you believe that knockwurst means "sausage whose skin cracks open when bitten"? "Kielbasa" is less complicated, being simply the Polish word for "sausage." Whatever type of sausage you use, the other ingredients in this soup make a good background for it.

¼ cup carrots, sliced
¼ cup celery, sliced
1½ cups sliced leeks (about 3 leeks cut into ½-inch pieces)
1½ cups diced potatoes
1 cup (about ¼ pound) thinly sliced kielbasa (if not available, use knockwurst)

1 teaspoon salt
½ teaspoon marjoram
¼ teaspoon chervil
⅛ teaspoon pepper
3 cups chicken broth

2 tablespoons flour
2 tablespoons butter or margarine

1. Combine all ingredients except flour and butter in cooker.
2. Cook on low 5 hours, or on high 3 hours.
3. To thicken soup, remove ¼ cup liquid and combine with flour and butter. Return mixture to cooker.

Yield: 5-6 servings

LAMB AND LIMA SOUP

1 pound lima beans
1½ pounds lamb shanks
2 tablespoons shortening
2 small onions, diced
2 carrots, diced
1-2 stalks celery, diced
1 clove garlic, crushed
1½ teaspoons salt
3 cups chicken stock
3 cups water

1. Soak beans overnight in water 1 inch above beans. Drain.
2. Heat shortening in skillet and brown meat well on all sides.
3. Place diced ingredients in cooker. Add beans, lamb, and other ingredients.
4. Cook on low 10 hours, or on automatic 7 hours.
5. Remove lamb shanks from cooker, strip meat from bones, and return meat to cooker.

Yield: 6-8 servings

Beef

This is the favorite meat of Americans, and with good reason. It's flavorful in itself, and it combines well with almost anything you can think of, from sour cream to dill pickles—and including apricots, curry powder and beer. Should you brown beef before adding it to your slow cooker? It all depends. With stewing beef, you may (beef bourguignon) or again you may not (beef en daube). With round steak (collops, Swiss steak), there's less need to brown than with fattier cuts (short ribs, oxtails). On the other hand, browning gives a nice texture to a pot roast. The best thing is to find out for yourself. You might want to try the same recipe twice, using browned meat once and unbrowned meat another time, and see which you prefer.

BASIC POT ROAST

1 3-4 pound rump or chuck roast
1 teaspoon salt
¼ teaspoon pepper
2 tablespoons shortening
3 medium potatoes, halved
3 medium carrots, cut into 2-inch pieces
2 medium onions, halved
½ cup water or beef broth

1. Season meat with salt and pepper.
2. Heat shortening in skillet and brown meat on all sides.
3. Place half of vegetables in bottom of cooker, add meat, then add other vegetables and liquid.
4. Cook on low 10-12 hours, on high 5 hours, or on automatic 6 hours.

Yield: 4-6 servings

POT ROAST WITH FRUIT

This unusual combination might have an accompaniment of curried rice or baked sweet potatoes. Serve with chicory and romaine salad.

¾ cup dried prunes, pitted
¾ cup dried apricots
½ teaspoon ginger
1 can light beer
1 4-pound chuck roast
2 tablespoons shortening

1 large onion, sliced thin
3 tablespoons brown sugar
½ teaspoon cinnamon
¼ cup honey

1. Soak dried fruits, with ginger, in beer for 1-2 hours.
2. Heat shortening in skillet and brown meat on all sides.
3. Transfer meat to cooker, add other ingredients, and pour marinated fruits over all.
4. Cook on low 10-12 hours, on high 5-6 hours, or on automatic 7 hours.

Yield: 6 servings

POT ROAST STROGANOFF

If you want to have good food named after you, try achieving fame as a diplomat or an opera singer. An otherwise unmemorable Russian count, one P. Stroganoff, gave his name to a classic filet of beef cooked with sour cream. Now the word is often used simply to indicate the use of sour cream, whether in a stew, a ragout, or—as here—with braised meat. This version is good served with noodles.

1 3-pound arm or chuck roast	2 teaspoons salt
1 tablespoon shortening	1 teaspoon caraway seed
4 ounces mushrooms, sliced	¼ teaspoon pepper
1 small onion, chopped	1 cup beef stock
½ cup ketchup	2 tablespoons butter or margarine
1 tablespoon Worcestershire sauce	2 tablespoons flour
	1 cup sour cream

1. Heat shortening in skillet and brown meat on all sides.
2. Combine other ingredients except last three in cooker and add browned meat.
3. Cook on low 8 hours.
4. Remove meat from cooker and keep warm.
5. In saucepan melt butter and add flour and ½ cup juices from cooker. Blend, then add sour cream. Return to cooker and stir well.
6. Pour sauce over meat.

Yield: 6-8 servings

BOURBON POT ROAST

1 4-5 pound rump roast	2 stalks celery, sliced
2 tablespoons shortening	2 teaspoons salt
	¼ teaspoon pepper
4 potatoes, quartered	1 bay leaf
2 carrots, cut in 3-inch pieces	½ teaspoon basil
	½ cup Bourbon whiskey

1. Heat shortening in skillet and brown meat on all sides.
2. Combine all ingredients in cooker and add browned meat.
3. Cook on low 10-12 hours, on high 5-6 hours, or on automatic 7 hours.

Yield: 8 servings

FRENCH POT ROAST

1 4-5 pound rump roast
¼ cup shortening
12 small carrots, left whole or cut in half
12 small white onions
½ pound fresh mushrooms, sliced
2 teaspoons salt
1 teaspoon celery seed
½ teaspoon nutmeg
½ teaspoon thyme
½ teaspoon crumbled bay leaves
¼ teaspoon tarragon
2 cups dry red wine

1. Heat shortening in skillet and brown meat on all sides.
2. Combine all ingredients in cooker and add browned meat. If wine does not cover, add water.
3. Cook on low 10-12 hours, on high 5-6 hours, or on automatic 7 hours.

Yield: 8 servings

STUFFED FLANK STEAK

In many localities, flank steak is known as London broil. This tasty version goes well with one of the cabbagey vegetables, such as Brussels sprouts or broccoli.

1 2-pound flank steak	1½ cups soft bread cubes
2 tablespoons butter or margarine	¾ teaspoon poultry seasoning
½ large onion, chopped	½ teaspoon salt
1 clove garlic, minced	⅛ teaspoon pepper
½ cup chopped mushrooms	1 egg, slightly beaten
¼ cup chopped parsley	½ cup water or bouillon

1. In a skillet heat the butter, add onion and garlic, and sauté until lightly browned. Add all other ingredients except meat and water, and stir well.
2. Spread the mixture on the steak. Roll up and secure with string. If steak is too wide for cooker, cut into two or more pieces.
3. Place steak in cooker and add liquid.
4. Cook on low 8-10 hours, or on automatic 6-7 hours.
5. To serve, cut into 1-inch slices.

Yield: 6 servings

SIMPLE BEEF STEW

2 pounds stewing beef,
  cut into 1-inch cubes
½ cup flour
2 teaspoons salt
½ teaspoon pepper
3 tablespoons shorten-
  ing
6 carrots, cut into
  1-inch pieces

1 cup sliced celery
1 large onion, sliced
1 clove garlic, minced
1 28-ounce can
  tomatoes
1 bay leaf
⅓ cup water

1. Mix flour, salt and pepper together and coat beef cubes with mixture.
2. Heat shortening in skillet and brown beef.
3. Combine all ingredients except water in cooker.
4. Add water to skillet, scrape brown bits from bottom, and add to cooker.
5. Cook on low 10-12 hours, on high 5 hours, or on automatic 6 hours.

Yield: 4-6 servings

PINK BEEF STEW

1 pound stewing beef,
   cut into 1-inch cubes
2 tablespoons flour
½ teaspoon salt
¼ teaspoon pepper
3 carrots, cut into
   1-inch pieces
1½ cups shredded
   cabbage

1 teaspoon salt
1 tablespoon parsley
   flakes
1 teaspoon Worcester-
   shire sauce
⅛ teaspoon caraway
   seed
1 can tomato soup
½ cup dry red wine

1. Mix flour, salt and pepper and coat beef cubes
   with mixture.
2. Place vegetables in cooker, top with meat and
   seasonings, and pour soup and wine over all.
3. Cook on low 8 hours, on high 4 hours, or on automatic 5 hours.

Yield: 4 servings

EPICUREAN BEEF CASSEROLE

2 pounds stewing beef, cut into 2-inch cubes

2 medium onions, sliced

1½ teaspoons salt

¼ teaspoon pepper

½ cup dry red wine

2 10½-ounce cans condensed consommé

½ cup fine dry bread crumbs

½ cup flour

1. Put all ingredients except crumbs and flour in cooker. Stir.
2. Mix crumbs with flour and add to cooker.
3. Cook on high 5-6 hours, or on automatic 7 hours.

Yield: 6 servings

BEEF STEW WITH BEER

2 pounds stewing beef, cut into 1-inch cubes
¼ cup flour
1 teaspoon salt
½ teaspoon pepper
3 slices bacon, diced
12 small onions
1 clove garlic, crushed
1 pound mushrooms, sliced
1 can beer
1 tablespoon soy sauce
1 tablespoon Worcestershire sauce
1 teaspoon thyme
½ teaspoon crumbled bay leaves

1. Mix flour, salt and pepper together and coat beef cubes with mixture.
2. Fry bacon bits until crisp; discard fat.
3. Mix together beer and seasonings.
4. Place beef, bacon, garlic, onions and mushrooms in cooker. Pour liquid mixture over them.
5. Cook on low 10 hours, on high 6 hours, or on automatic 7 hours.

Yield: 6 servings

BEEF CUBES, CURRIED

2 pounds stewing beef, cut in 1½-inch pieces
⅓ cup flour
⅓ cup shortening
1 large onion, sliced
1 clove garlic, minced
2 8-ounce cans tomato sauce
2-3 teaspoons curry powder

1. Coat beef cubes with flour.
2. Heat shortening in skillet and sauté beef.
3. Combine all ingredients in cooker.
4. Cook on low 8 hours.

Yield: 6-8 servings

BEEF GOULASH

In Hungarian, *gulyas* means "shepherd," though some of the more complex versions of the dish now current are more at home in high-style Viennese restaurants. Good served with gnocchi or risotto.

2 pounds stewing beef, cut into 1½-inch chunks

2 tablespoons flour

3 large onions, chopped

1 clove garlic, minced

2 teaspoons marjoram

2 teaspoons lemon rind, finely chopped

1 teaspoon caraway seed

1½ teaspoons salt

2 tablespoons paprika (the sweet Hungarian variety, if obtainable)

1 tablespoon tomato paste

1 cup water

1 cup sour cream

1. Dredge beef with flour.
2. Combine all ingredients except sour cream in cooker.
3. Cook on low 8-10 hours, or on high 5-6 hours.
4. Before serving, stir sour cream into sauce and heat.

Yield: 4-6 servings

SWEET-SOUR BEEF STEW

2 pounds stewing beef, cut into 1½-inch cubes

1 cup chopped onion

¼ cup flour

6 large carrots, cut into ¾-inch pieces

1 teaspoon salt

¼ cup brown sugar

⅛ teaspoon pepper

½ cup vinegar

4 tablespoons shortening

1 tablespoon Worcestershire sauce

1. Mix flour, salt and pepper and dredge beef with mixture.
2. Heat shortening in skillet and brown meat well.
3. Place carrots in bottom of cooker. Add meat and onions.
4. Combine remaining ingredients and add to cooker.
5. Cook 7-8 hours on automatic.

Yield: 6 servings

BEEF AND ARTICHOKES

1½ pounds stewing beef, cut into 1-inch cubes
¼ cup flour
1 teaspoon salt
½ teaspoon pepper
2 tablespoons shortening
8 small white onions
8 large mushrooms, sliced
½ teaspoon dill weed
½ teaspoon basil
1 15-ounce can tomato sauce
½ cup red wine
1 package frozen artichoke hearts, thawed

1. Mix flour, salt and pepper together and coat beef cubes with mixture.
2. Heat shortening in skillet and sauté beef.
3. Combine all ingredients except artichokes in cooker.
4. Cook on low 9-10 hours.
5. Add thawed artichoke hearts and cook 1 hour longer.

Yield: 4 servings

BEEF BOURGUIGNON

The name indicates an origin in the Burgundy region of France. More particularly, the term "bourguignon" (or "à la bourguignonne"—"in the style of the Burgundy housewife") means braised meat cooked with onions, mushrooms and red wine. Like many other stews, it can be made a day or two in advance and reheated. The traditional accompaniment is small boiled potatoes sprinkled with parsley.

1 cup dry red wine
2 tablespoons olive oil
1 large onion, sliced
½ teaspoon thyme
2 tablespoons chopped parsley
1 bay leaf
¼ teaspoon pepper
2 pounds stewing beef, cut into 1½-inch cubes

3 slices bacon (thick-cut, if possible), diced
12 small white onions
½ pound mushrooms, sliced
2 cloves garlic, minced
1 teaspoon salt

1. Combine first seven ingredients, mix well, and add beef.
2. Marinate at least 3 hours (overnight if refrigerated).
3. Drain meat, reserving marinade.
4. In skillet, sauté bacon and remove. Brown meat in bacon fat.
5. Combine beef, bacon, vegetables and seasonings in cooker. Pour over enough of the marinade to cover.
6. Cook on low 8-10 hours.

Yield: 4 servings

BEEF EN DAUBE

A *daubière* is a type of French casserole, which used to be made with a very deep lid to hold live charcoal and ashes. Today the word *daube* refers to almost any kind of meat casserole dish covered and cooked for a long time. Though this version requires marinating before cooking, it is well worth the trouble.

1½ cups dry red wine
2 tablespoons olive oil
2 teaspoons salt
¼ teaspoon pepper
½ teaspoon sage or thyme
1 bay leaf, crumbled
2 cloves garlic
2 cups onions, thinly sliced
2 cups carrots, thinly sliced

2 pounds stewing beef, cut into 2-inch cubes
6 slices bacon (thick-cut, if possible), cut into 1-inch pieces
1 cup sliced mushrooms
1 28-ounce can tomatoes, drained and chopped
flour

1. Combine first six ingredients in large bowl. Add crushed garlic, vegetables and beef.
2. Marinate, stirring occasionally, for at least 4 hours (overnight, if refrigerated).
3. Simmer bacon 10 minutes in water. Drain.
4. Drain marinade, reserving it in a bowl. Separate meat from vegetables. Dredge meat with flour.
5. In cooker, alternate layers as follows: bacon, marinade vegetables, mushrooms, tomatoes and meat. Pour over marinade liquid to cover.
6. Cook on high 3 hours, then switch to low 8 hours. Or cook on automatic 12 hours.

Yield: 8 servings

COLLOPS

This term, in English use since the fourteenth century, originally meant bacon; the Monday before Ash Wednesday was known as Collop Monday, which a lot of people celebrated by eating bacon and eggs. The term now means simply thin slices of meat. Try it with creamed onions or puréed spinach.

2 pounds top round, cut into serving pieces ⅜-inch thick
1 onion, chopped
½ teaspoon salt
½ teaspoon pepper
½ teaspoon thyme
½ teaspoon marjoram
½ teaspoon savory
1 tablespoon capers

2 tablespoons chopped parsley
1 cup beef stock

6 anchovies, coarsely chopped
¼ cup bread crumbs
1 tablespoon butter

1 lemon, thinly sliced toast triangles

1. Combine meat, onion and seasoning in cooker. Pour in beef stock.
2. Cook on low 8 hours, or on high 3-4 hours.
3. Remove meat from cooker and stir in anchovies, crumbs and butter.
4. Serve meat on toast triangles, pour sauce over them and garnish with lemon.

Yield: 6 servings

BRAISED SHORT RIBS

Good with baked or mashed potatoes. For a change, serve with slices of fried cornmeal mush.

3 pounds beef short ribs, cut up
1 cup flour
1 teaspoon salt
½ teaspoon pepper
2 tablespoons shortening

2 onions, sliced
1 bay leaf
½ teaspoon whole allspice
1 cup beef broth

1. Mix flour, salt and pepper, and coat beef ribs with mixture.
2. Heat shortening in skillet and brown meat well.
3. Combine all ingredients in cooker.
4. Cook on low 8-10 hours or on high 4-6 hours.
5. Before serving, remove bay leaf and allspice.

Yield: 6-8 servings

Note: Since short ribs tend to be rather fat, skim off excess after cooking, or refrigerate overnight and then do so.

CORNED BEEF AND CABBAGE

A specialty long associated with Irish Americans—perhaps because of the comic-strip character Jiggs. Serve with horseradish or Dijon mustard.

3 pounds corned beef brisket
1 large onion, quartered
1 head of cabbage, cut into small wedges
¼ teaspoon pepper
2 tablespoons vinegar
2 tablespoons sugar
1 cup water

1. Combine ingredients in cooker, with cabbage on top. Cut meat in pieces if necessary to fit in cooker.
2. Cook on low 10-12 hours, or on high 6-7 hours.

Yield: 4 servings

OXTAIL STEW

As *Larousse Gastronomique* puts it: "The caudal appendage of the ox's body is a very tasty bit." A good side dish with this stew is noodles sprinkled with poppy seeds. Have some good bread to sop up the plentiful gravy.

2 pounds oxtails, disjointed	4 carrots, quartered
1 medium onion, sliced	1 teaspoon salt
1 cup coarsely sliced celery	¼ teaspoon pepper
½ cup chopped green pepper	½ bay leaf, crumbled
4 medium potatoes, quartered	1 tablespoon Worcestershire sauce
	1 can condensed beef broth

1. Combine ingredients in cooker, stirring well.
2. Cook on low 8-10 hours, or on high 5-6 hours.

Yield: 6 servings

Note: Skim fat off after cooking, or refrigerate and then do so.

OXTAILS IN WINE

3 pounds oxtails,
 disjointed
4 tablespoons flour
1 tablespoon salt
½ teaspoon pepper
3 tablespoons shorten-
 ing

6 small white onions
6 medium potatoes,
 quartered
6 carrots, sliced
2 leeks, sliced
1 cup beef stock
1 cup dry red wine

1. Mix together flour, salt, and pepper and coat oxtails with mixture.
2. Heat shortening in skillet and brown oxtails, discarding fat.
3. Combine all ingredients in cooker.
4. Cook on low 7-9 hours, or on automatic 4-5 hours.

Yield: 6 servings

BOILED BEEF DINNER

If you want to serve this old American meal in the customary way, each person should begin with a cup of broth from the pot. Then slice the brisket and serve it with the vegetables. Accompaniments consist of horseradish, sour pickles, and coarse salt (the kosher kind is good, if you can get it).

1 4-pound fresh brisket	½ teaspoon pepper
1 onion stuck with 2 cloves	1 teaspoon rosemary
1 bay leaf	1 cup water
1 clove garlic	6 carrots, sliced
1 stalk celery, cut into 2-3 pieces	6 turnips, diced
1½ tablespoons salt	10 medium potatoes, with skins left on
	1 small head cabbage, cut into chunks

1. Place beef in cooker and add next eight ingredients. Cut meat in pieces if necessary to fit in cooker.
2. Cook on low 10-12 hours.
3. Add vegetables and cook on high 1-2 hours, or on automatic 3 hours.

Yield: 8-10 servings

CHOLENT

This traditional Jewish dish has been traced back to medieval Italy. By that time rabbinical law forbade any work (including cooking) on the Sabbath—that is, from sundown on Friday to sundown on Saturday. A housewife would assemble all the components of this stew and put it on to cook late Friday afternoon. It would be ready to enjoy when the family came home from Sabbath services the next day. The name may come from *shule ende*—German for "end of synagogue [services]."

½ pound lima beans
3 pounds fresh beef
   brisket
1½ teaspoons salt
¼ teaspoon pepper
½ teaspoon paprika

1 small clove garlic,
   cut in two
3 onions, sliced
¼ cup shortening
   (chicken fat is
   traditional)
½ pound barley

1. Soak beans overnight.
2. Rub meat with salt, pepper, paprika and garlic.
3. Heat shortening in skillet; brown onions and remove. Brown meat in fat.
4. Put meat in cooker, cutting into pieces if necessary. Add remaining ingredients.
5. Cook on low 11-12 hours, or on automatic 7 hours.

Yield: 6-8 servings

POT AU FEU

Generations of French housewives have fed their families with this staple—the "pot on the fire" that rests constantly on the stove and into which all manner of odds and ends may be added.

1 pound beef bones or veal knuckle
8 carrots, cut in half
8 medium onions, quartered
6 small turnips, quartered
6 parsnips, halved
6 medium potatoes, halved
½ cabbage, cut into chunks

1 tablespoon salt
* bouquet garni consisting of 2 sprigs parsley, 2 stalks sliced celery, 2 bay leaves, and 12 peppercorns
1 pound link sausages
1-2 pounds boneless chuck, round, or fresh brisket
bouillon

1. Place bones and next seven ingredients in cooker. Add bouquet garni.
2. In skillet, brown sausage links, discarding fat. Add sausage and beef to cooker.
3. Add enough bouillon to cover food.
4. Cook on low 10 hours.
5. Remove bouquet garni.

Yield: 6-8 servings

* *See pages 33–34.*

MEAT LOAF

2 eggs, beaten
¾ cup milk
2 teaspoons salt
½ teaspoon pepper
3 slices bread, crumbled
2 pounds ground chuck
½ cup chopped onion
¼ cup chopped green pepper
¼ cup chopped celery
½ cup ketchup
½ cup additional ketchup

1. Mix eggs, milk, seasonings and bread crumbs; allow to soften.
2. Combine crumb mixture with all other ingredients except the last, and shape into a loaf.
3. Place loaf in cooker and cover with additional ketchup.
4. Cook on high 1 hour, then switch to low 8-9 hours. Or cook on automatic 7 hours.

Yield: 6-8 servings

THREE-MEAT LOAF

1½ pounds ground
    chuck
¼ pound ground pork
¼ pound ground veal
2 eggs, beaten
1 cup bread crumbs
½ cup water
1 package onion-soup
    mix

1 tablespoon Worces-
    tershire sauce
1 teaspoon salt
½ teaspoon oregano
½ teaspoon thyme
1 8-ounce can tomato
    sauce

1. Combine all ingredients except tomato sauce. Form into a loaf.
2. Place loaf in cooker and pour tomato sauce on top.
3. Cook on high 1 hour, then switch to low 8-9 hours. Or cook on automatic 7 hours.

Yield: 6-8 servings

SWISS STEAK

2 pounds round steak, cut into serving pieces

1 teaspoon salt

⅛ teaspoon pepper

1 large onion, sliced (or 1 package onion-soup mix)

1 16-ounce can tomatoes

1. Combine all ingredients in cooker.
2. Cook on low 6-10 hours or on high 3-4 hours.

Yield: 3-4 servings

SWEDISH MEAT BALLS

The large economy size specified here are fine for a
main-dish meal, served with noodles or rice. Smaller
meat balls make delicious cocktail snacks.

1½ cups bread crumbs	¼ teaspoon allspice
1 cup milk	⅛ teaspoon nutmeg
1½ pounds ground chuck	2 tablespoons shortening
2 eggs, beaten	1 can beef broth
1 medium onion, finely chopped	¾ teaspoon dill weed
1½ teaspoons salt	⅛ teaspoon pepper

1. Soak bread crumbs in milk 5 minutes.
2. Combine crumb mixture with meat, eggs and next
   four ingredients. Shape into balls about an inch
   in diameter.
3. Heat shortening in skillet and brown meat balls.
4. Place meat balls in cooker and add broth, dill
   weed and pepper.
5. Cook on low 4 hours.

Yield: 3 dozen meat balls

GROUND BEEF STROGANOFF

2 pounds ground beef
2 tablespoons shortening
2 medium onions, chopped
2 cloves garlic, minced
½ pound mushrooms, sliced
2 teaspoons salt

¼ teaspoon pepper
1 tablespoon Worcestershire sauce
3 tablespoons tomato paste
⅓ cup dry red wine (optional)
1 cup beef broth

1 cup sour cream

1. Heat shortening in skillet and brown beef, discarding fat.
2. Combine all ingredients except sour cream in cooker.
3. Cook on low 6-8 hours.
4. Before serving, add sour cream to sauce and heat.

Yield: 6-8 servings

NOODLE-CORN CASSEROLE

1 pound ground beef
2 tablespoons shortening
1 medium onion, sliced very thin
1½ teaspoons salt
⅛ teaspoon pepper
1 teaspoon Worcestershire sauce

1 can condensed cream of celery soup
1 soup can water
1 1-pound can cream-style corn
2 cups (about half an 8-ounce package) fine noodles

chopped parsley

1. Heat shortening in skillet and brown beef, discarding fat.
2. Combine all ingredients except noodles and parsley in cooker.
3. Cook on high 3 hours.
4. Add noodles and cook until done (about 15 minutes).
5. Serve with chopped parsley.

Yield: 4 servings

BEEF AND RICE CASSEROLE

1 pound ground beef
2 tablespoons shortening
1 small onion, sliced very thin
½ cup sliced celery
1 teaspoon soy sauce
⅛ teaspoon oregano

1 can condensed cream of chicken soup
1 cup cooked rice
toasted slivered almonds

1. Heat shortening in skillet and brown beef, discarding fat.
2. Combine all ingredients except rice and almonds in cooker.
3. Cook on high 3 hours.
4. Add cooked rice.
5. Serve with toasted almonds.

Yield: 6 servings

BORDER CASSEROLE

1½ pounds ground beef
2 tablespoons shortening
1 medium onion, chopped
½ cup chopped celery
2 1-pound cans baked beans
1 8-ounce can tomato sauce
1 cup grated Cheddar cheese
1½ teaspoons chili powder
¼ teaspoon oregano

1. Heat shortening in skillet and brown beef, discarding fat.
2. Combine all ingredients in cooker, stirring well.
3. Cook on low 4-6 hours.

Yield: 8 servings

STUFFED CABBAGE

12 large cabbage leaves
1½ pounds ground beef
⅓ cup quick-cooking rolled oats
1 small onion, minced
2 tablespoons chopped parsley
1 egg
½ cup beef stock
1 teaspoon salt

⅛ teaspoon pepper
1 cup tomato juice
3 tablespoons lemon juice
¼ cup sweet red wine
3 tablespoons brown sugar
½ bay leaf, crumbled
1 teaspoon salt
¼ teaspoon pepper

1. Cook the cabbage leaves in boiling salted water to cover about 5 minutes, until just tender.
2. In bowl, combine ground beef and next seven ingredients, mixing well.
3. Separate stuffing into twelve equal portions. Place one portion on each leaf, folding to make a compact roll. (If necessary, fasten rolls together with toothpicks.)
4. Place cabbage rolls in cooker.
5. In bowl, mix together tomato juice and next six ingredients. Pour sauce over cabbage rolls.
6. Cook on high 4-5 hours, or on automatic 5-6 hours.

Yield: 6 servings

STUFFED PEPPERS

6 medium green pep-
pers, tops removed
and seeded
1 tablespoon shortening
1 pound ground beef
1 cup cooked rice
1 small onion, chopped

1 teaspoon salt
⅛ teaspoon pepper
½ teaspoon basil
¼ cup ketchup

1 8-ounce can tomato
sauce

1. Heat shortening in skillet and brown beef.
2. Combine meat and next six ingredients in bowl. Stuff green peppers about two-thirds full.
3. Arrange peppers in cooker, with two or three on bottom and others placed above them. (Sprinkle leftover stuffing on top.)
4. Pour tomato sauce into cooker.
5. Cook on low 6-7 hours, or on high 3-4 hours.

Yield: 6 servings

SPAGHETTI SAUCE

For a change from the usual spaghetti, try green (spinach) spaghetti or noodles. Try grating your own Parmesan or Romano cheese. This is easily done if you put smallish chunks into a blender.

2 pounds ground beef
2 tablespoons shortening
1 cup chopped onion
1 cup chopped green pepper
2 cloves garlic, crushed
1 cup chopped mushrooms (optional)

2 28-ounce cans tomatoes
1 6-ounce can tomato paste
2 teaspoons salt
3 teaspoons oregano
½ teaspoon rosemary
¼ teaspoon thyme

1. Heat shortening in skillet and brown beef, discarding fat.
2. Combine all ingredients in cooker, stirring well.
3. Cook on low 10-12 hours, on high 5-6 hours, or on automatic 6 hours.

Yield: 2 quarts sauce

CHILI CON CARNE

Opinions about chili—like those on clam chowder—tend to be rather passionate. One school of thought, for instance, believes that it should be made with chunks of stewing beef rather than the more common ground beef. Some like it searingly hot, others on the mild side. Wash it down with milk? Those who do are scorned by the beer-drinkers. This is a rather middle-of-the-road version, which you may modify as you choose. Serve with oyster crackers and a cooling dessert such as lemon sherbet.

2 pounds ground beef	1 teaspoon ground cumin
2 tablespoons shortening	½ teaspoon cayenne pepper
2 cups chopped onion	½ cup beef stock
2 cloves garlic, crushed	1 28-ounce can tomatoes
3 tablespoons chili powder	3 1-pound cans red kidney beans
1 teaspoon salt	
1 teaspoon paprika	
1 teaspoon oregano	

1. Heat shortening in skillet and brown beef, discarding fat.
2. Combine all ingredients in cooker, stirring well.
3. Cook on low 8-10 hours, on high 5 hours, or on automatic 6 hours.

Yield: 8-10 servings

BARBECUED SPOONBURGERS

Known also as sloppy joes, these are usually served on warmed hamburger buns. Good too over noodles or rice.

1½ pounds ground beef	1 teaspoon salt
2 tablespoons shortening	½ teaspoon paprika
½ cup chopped onion	⅛ teaspoon pepper
½ cup diced celery	1 6-ounce can tomato paste
½ green pepper, chopped	¾ cup water
1 clove garlic, minced	2 tablespoons vinegar
1 tablespoon Worcestershire sauce	2 teaspoons brown sugar
½ cup ketchup	1 teaspoon dry mustard

1. Heat shortening in skillet and brown beef, discarding fat.
2. Combine all ingredients in cooker, stirring well.
3. Cook on low 6-8 hours, or on high 3-4 hours.

Yield: 8-10 servings

SLUMGULLION

Not elegant, but good. The name may have been invented by hobos to refer to watery tea or coffee. Spoon over hamburger buns or onion rolls.

2 pounds ground beef
2 tablespoons shortening
1 large onion, chopped
1 clove garlic, minced
1 cup chopped celery
1 envelope spaghetti-sauce mix

1 18-ounce can tomato juice
1 1-pound can whole-kernel corn

½ cup chopped dill pickle

1. Heat shortening in skillet and brown beef, discarding fat.
2. Combine all ingredients except pickle in cooker, stirring well.
3. Cook on low 6-8 hours, or on high 3-4 hours.
4. Stir in chopped dill pickle.

Yield: 8 servings

EASY BEEF DINNER

1 cup cooked beef, cut into 1-inch cubes
1 medium onion, sliced
½ cup uncooked rice
1½ teaspoons salt
⅛ teaspoon pepper
1 tablespoon Worcestershire sauce
1 1-pound can tomatoes, with juice
½ cup water

1. Combine all ingredients in cooker.
2. Cook on high 5-6 hours, or on automatic 7-8 hours.

Yield: 4 servings

Note: You can vary this by using just about any kind of leftover meat.

Veal and Lamb

Both of these meats—somewhat neglected in American kitchens—are extremely compatible with slow cooking. Although several of the veal recipes included here suggest browning the meat before adding it to the cooker, try adding it unbrowned for a change, or if you're in a hurry. As it's a lean meat, you won't be troubled by excess fat. Italian cuisine makes good use of veal; try veal scallopini or osso buco. With lamb, trim off any fat you can before cooking. This meat is a favorite in Greek and Middle Eastern cooking. Included here are just a few of the many possibilities for slow cookery, among them Arabian lamb stew and lamb and artichokes, Greek style. Anyway, don't overlook veal and lamb.

VEAL POT ROAST

1 3-4 pound veal rump roast or rolled leg
1 tablespoon dry mustard
1 teaspoon poultry seasoning
1 tablespoon brown sugar
1 tablespoon salt
¼ teaspoon pepper
1 tablespoon flour
2 tablespoons shortening
1 onion, thinly sliced
¼ cup water
1 bay leaf, crumbled
3 tablespoons cider vinegar

1. Mix mustard with next five ingredients in small bowl and rub well into roast.
2. Heat shortening in skillet and brown roast well on all sides.
3. Place meat in cooker and cover with onion slices.
4. Mix last three ingredients together and pour over roast.
5. Cook on low 6-8 hours, or on high 3-4 hours.

Yield: 6-8 servings

VEAL GOULASH

1 pound boneless veal,
    cut into 1-inch cubes
3 tablespoons flour
1 teaspoon salt
⅛ teaspoon pepper
2 tablespoons shorten-
    ing
1 medium onion, thinly
    sliced

1 tablespoon paprika
    (the sweet Hungarian
    variety if obtainable)
1 teaspoon thyme
1 8-ounce can tomato
    sauce
½ cup tomato juice

½ cup sour cream

1. Mix flour, salt and pepper and coat veal with
   mixture.
2. Heat shortening in skillet; sauté veal.
3. Combine all ingredients except sour cream in
   cooker.
4. Cook on low 8-10 hours, on high 5 hours, or on
   automatic 6 hours.
5. Before serving, add sour cream.

Yield: 4 servings

VEAL ROAST WITH ROSEMARY

Like chicken and tarragon, veal and rosemary seem to have a natural affinity. Try serving this roast with a fairly tangy vegetable, such as cauliflower or broccoli with lemon butter.

1 3-pound veal rump roast, boned, rolled, and tied	3 medium onions, quartered
2 tablespoons flour	3 carrots, cut into 1-inch pieces
1½ teaspoons salt	1 clove garlic, minced
⅛ teaspoon pepper	1 tablespoon rosemary
2 tablespoons shortening	¼ cup water
	¼ cup white wine

1. Sprinkle roast with salt and pepper and dredge with flour.
2. Heat shortening in skillet and brown roast well on all sides.
3. Place onions and carrots in bottom of cooker. Add meat.
4. Mix last four ingredients together and pour into cooker.
5. Cook on low 8-9 hours.

Yield: 6 servings

VEAL AND PEPPERS

1½ pounds boneless veal, cut into 2-inch cubes

3 green peppers, cut into quarters

2 onions, thinly sliced

½ pound mushrooms, sliced

1 teaspoon salt

½ teaspoon basil

1 28-ounce can tomatoes

1. Combine all ingredients in cooker.
2. Cook on low 7 hours, on high 4 hours, or on automatic 5 hours.

Yield: 4 servings

VEAL SCALLOPINI

Though this dish is often served with rice, try it with buttered new potatoes instead. Another good accompaniment is very thin spaghetti sprinkled with grated Parmesan cheese.

2 pounds boneless veal, cut into thin pieces about 1 inch long and ½ inch thick
½ cup flour
½ teaspoon salt
⅛ teaspoon pepper
⅓ cup shortening
1 cup chopped onion
1 clove garlic, minced
¾ cup mushrooms, sliced
1 28-ounce can tomatoes, drained (reserve liquid)
1½ teaspoons salt
1 teaspoon basil
½ teaspoon sugar
⅛ teaspoon pepper

1. Mix flour, salt and pepper and coat veal pieces with mixture.
2. Heat shortening in skillet and sauté veal. Remove meat to cooker.
3. Drain tomato juice from canned tomatoes into skillet and scrape up brown bits. Add this and all remaining ingredients to cooker.
4. Cook on low 8 hours, or on automatic 3½ hours.

Yield: 5-6 servings

SAVORY VEAL WITH OLIVES

2 pounds boneless veal, cut into 2-inch cubes
3 tablespoons flour
1½ teaspoons salt
12 small white onions
¼ pound mushrooms, sliced
1 cup pitted ripe olives, sliced
1 8-ounce can tomato sauce
1 teaspoon chili powder
½ bay leaf, crumbled
½ teaspoon marjoram
¼ teaspoon thyme
⅛ teaspoon pepper
2 Italian sweet sausages
2 Italian hot sausages

1. Sprinkle veal with salt and dredge with flour.
2. Place onions in cooker and add meat.
3. Mix next eight ingredients together and add to cooker.
4. Slip sausages out of casings, brown lightly, and add to cooker.
5. Cook on high 4 hours, or on automatic 5 hours.

Yield: 6 servings

LEMON VEAL

A delicate combination of flavors, nicely accompanied by green beans with almonds and a salad of Boston or Bibb lettuce.

3 pounds boneless veal, cut into 1½-inch cubes
3 tablespoons flour
2 slices bacon, diced
1 small lemon, sliced
1 clove garlic, minced
1 teaspoon salt
½ teaspoon marjoram

1 teaspoon Worcestershire sauce
½ cup chicken broth
¼ cup dry vermouth
1 bay leaf, crumbled

1 can artichoke hearts, drained

1 lemon, sliced very thin

1. Fry bacon bits until crisp. Remove.
2. Dredge veal with flour and brown in bacon fat.
3. Combine all ingredients except artichokes and lemon garnish in cooker.
4. Cook on low 8 hours, on high 4-6 hours, or on automatic 5 hours.
5. Add artichoke hearts and heat.
6. Serve garnished with very thin slices of lemon.

Yield: 6 servings

OSSO BUCO

A specialty of northern Italy, where good cattle are raised. The name means "hollow bones."

3 whole shanks of
 veal, cut by butcher
 into 3-inch pieces
3 tablespoons flour
½ cup shortening
1 onion, sliced thin
1 clove garlic, crushed
2 small carrots, sliced
 thin
1 cup diced celery

1½ tablespoons chopped
 parsley
1 bay leaf
1 tablespoon grated
 lemon peel
1½ teaspoons salt
¼ teaspoon pepper
1 cup dry white wine
1 28-ounce can toma-
 toes, drained (re-
 serve liquid)

1. Dredge the shanks with flour.
2. Heat shortening in skillet and brown the shanks on all sides.
3. Combine all ingredients in cooker, using tomato liquid just to cover if necessary.
4. Cook on low 8-10 hours, or on high 4-6 hours.

Yield: 6 servings

CHOP SUEY

Most of us are now aware that this is more an American than a Chinese invention. The name at least is Chinese (Cantonese *shap sui*, meaning "mixed bits"). And the concoction is here to stay, whatever its origins.

1 pound boneless veal, cut into 1-inch cubes

1 pound boneless pork, cut into 1-inch cubes

2 tablespoons shortening

4 cups thinly sliced celery

1 cup sliced mushrooms

1 can chicken soup with rice

1 can cream of mushroom soup

2 tablespoons soy sauce

1 quart water

1 can crisp Chinese noodles

1. Heat shortening in skillet and sauté meat.
2. Combine all ingredients except noodles in cooker.
3. Cook on low 6-8 hours, or on high 3-4 hours.
4. Serve over Chinese noodles.

Yield: 6-8 servings

LAMB STEW

Good with fresh whole wheat bread and sweet butter. Serve chocolate or butterscotch pudding for dessert.

3 pounds boneless lamb, cut into 1½-inch cubes
3 tablespoons flour
2 teaspoons salt
¼ teaspoon pepper
3 tablespoons shortening
1 green pepper, cubed

1 onion, chopped
3 carrots, sliced
6 potatoes, quartered
1 cup sliced celery
½ teaspoon sage, crumbled
1 1-pound can tomatoes
1 cup water

1. Mix flour, salt and pepper and coat lamb with mixture.
2. Heat shortening in skillet and sauté meat.
3. Combine all ingredients in cooker.
4. Cook on high 2 hours, then switch to low 10 hours. Or cook on automatic 7-8 hours.

Yield: 6-8 servings

LAMB STEW WITH CAULIFLOWER

2 pounds boneless lamb, cut into 1½-inch cubes
2 medium onions, chopped
1 small cauliflower, cut into florets
1 clove garlic, minced
1 tablespoon chopped parsley
1½ teaspoons salt
¼ teaspoon pepper
1 6-ounce can tomato paste
1 cup white wine

1. Combine all ingredients in cooker.
2. Cook on high for 5-6 hours, or on automatic for 7-8 hours.

Yield: 4-6 servings

LAMB STROGANOFF

2 pounds boneless lamb, cut into 1½-inch cubes
½ cup chopped onion
1 clove garlic, minced
1 tablespoon paprika
1 teaspoon salt
½ teaspoon pepper
1 16-ounce can tomato sauce
¼ teaspoon rosemary
1 teaspoon Worcestershire sauce

1 cup sour cream

1. Combine all ingredients except sour cream in cooker.
2. Cook on low 6-8 hours, or on high 4-5 hours.
3. Before serving, add sour cream to sauce and heat.

Yield: 4-6 servings

ARABIAN LAMB STEW

1½ pounds boneless lamb, cut into 1-inch cubes

4 tablespoons shortening

¼ cup dried apricot halves

¼ cup dried peach halves

¼ cup pitted prunes, chopped

¼ cup seedless raisins

1½ teaspoons salt

¼ teaspoon pepper

¼ teaspoon coriander

¼ teaspoon cloves

½ cup dry white wine

¼ cup water

3 tablespoons pignoli nuts (optional)

salted almonds

1. In skillet, heat shortening and sauté lamb until brown.
2. Place meat and dried fruits in cooker.
3. In bowl, combine salt and next five ingredients. Pour into cooker.
4. Cook on low 8-9 hours.
5. Add pignoli and heat.
6. Serve garnished with salted almonds.

Yield: 4-5 servings

LAMB AND ARTICHOKES, GREEK STYLE

2-3 pounds boneless
lamb, cut into 2-inch
cubes
2 medium onions,
sliced
1 teaspoon salt
½ teaspoon dried mint
½ teaspoon anise seed
(if not available, use
rosemary)

¼ teaspoon pepper
2 tablespoons lemon
juice
½ cup dry white wine
½ cup beef stock

2 packages frozen
artichokes, thawed

1. Combine all ingredients except artichokes in cooker.
2. Cook on high 3½ hours.
3. Add artichokes and cook 1 hour longer.

Yield: 4-6 servings

BAKED LAMB SHANKS

If you want to impress those for whom you're cooking, you might announce that they're about to eat *podarakia arniou*—a rather musical, Greek way of saying "lamb shanks." Broccoli goes well with this, and you might serve honey-drenched Greek pastry for dessert.

3 lamb shanks, cracked
1 garlic clove, split
1½ teaspoons salt
¼ teaspoon pepper
1 medium onion, thinly sliced
2 small carrots, cut into thin strips
2 stalks celery, cut into thin 2-inch strips
2 bay leaves, crumbled
1 teaspoon oregano
1 teaspoon thyme
½ cup dry white wine
1 8-ounce can tomato sauce

1. Rub lamb with garlic and season with salt and pepper.
2. Place onion, carrots and celery in bottom of cooker. Add meat and all other ingredients.
3. Cook on low 8-10 hours, or on high 4-6 hours.

Yield: 4-6 servings

LAMB WITH PINTO BEANS

1 cup pinto beans
2 slices bacon, diced
2 lamb shanks, cracked
2 tablespoons flour
1 teaspoon salt
¼ teaspoon pepper
1 cup sliced mush-
rooms
½ cup sliced leeks
(optional)

1 teaspoon prepared
mustard
¾ teaspoon dry mustard
¾ teaspoon sage
¾ teaspoon basil
¼ teaspoon thyme
1 clove garlic, minced
1½ cups water

1. Soak beans overnight. Drain.
2. Fry bacon bits until crisp.
3. Mix flour, salt and pepper and coat lamb shanks.
4. Sauté lamb in bacon fat until brown on all sides.
5. Arrange ingredients in cooker as follows: half of
   beans, half of bacon, 1 lamb shank, and half of
   other ingredients (except water); add remaining
   beans, bacon, shank, and rest of other ingredients.
   Cover with water.
6. Cook on low 10 hours, or on automatic 7 hours.

Yield: 4 servings

BIGOS

A variation of a well-known Polish stew. After big hunting parties, Polish nobles liked to eat pots of bigos washed down with ample amounts of vodka.

3 pounds boneless lamb, cut into 2-inch cubes

3 tablespoons shortening

1½ teaspoons salt

¼ teaspoon pepper

½ pound bacon, diced

1 medium cabbage, cut into chunks

2 large onions, chopped

2 large tart apples, quartered, pared, cored and chopped

1 cup beef stock

½ kielbasa or knockwurst, sliced thin

fresh chopped dill weed (if not available, use dried)

1. Heat shortening in skillet and brown lamb well.
2. In cooker, alternate layers as follows: cabbage, onion, apple, lamb (seasoned with salt and pepper), and bacon. Pour stock over all.
3. Cook on low 6 hours.
4. Add sausage and cook 2 hours more.
5. Serve garnished with dill.

Yield: 6-8 servings

LAMB CURRY

2 pounds boneless lamb,
cut into 1-inch cubes
1 large onion, chopped
2 stalks celery, chopped
½ cup raisins
2 tablespoons curry
powder

1 teaspoon salt
¼ teaspoon pepper
¼ teaspoon ginger
¼ teaspoon tumeric
(optional)
1 cup chicken stock

1 cup yogurt

1. Combine all ingredients except yogurt in cooker.
2. Cook on low 8-9 hours, or on high 4-5 hours.
3. Add yogurt and heat.

Yield: 4-6 servings

Pork

According to an American folk song, one man's dream of plenty was a marvelous town where

Little roasted piggies go running
through the city streets
Inquiring so politely if a slice of ham
you'd like to eat.

Because salt pork and ham were often the only meats available for many months before the days of refrigeration, they have often been associated with a well-stocked pantry. We speak of a full larder (from "lard") and "living high off the hog." Like beef, pork combines with a multitude of good things, especially fruits. It is rich in fat, though, so in most cases you'll probably want to brown it before placing it in your slow cooker. Otherwise make sure you can skim off excess fat during or after cooking.

PORK POT ROAST

1 4-pound loin-end pork roast
1 clove garlic, cut in slivers
2 medium onions, sliced thin
1 teaspoon salt
¼ teaspoon pepper
2 bay leaves, crumbled
1 teaspoon sage
1 cup hot water

1. Make tiny slits in meat and insert slivers of garlic. Place meat in broiler pan and broil 20 minutes, or until browned; discard fat. Cut meat in pieces to fit in cooker.
2. Put one sliced onion in bottom of cooker. Top with pork and sprinkle with salt, pepper, bay leaves and sage. Arrange remaining sliced onion on meat and add water.
3. Cook on low 8-10 hours.

Yield: 6-8 servings

BRAISED PORK CHOPS

6-8 lean pork chops, cut about 1 inch thick
⅓ cup flour
1 teaspoon salt
1 teaspoon dry mustard
½ teaspoon garlic salt
2 tablespoons shortening
1 can cream of chicken soup

1. Mix flour, salt, mustard and garlic salt, and dredge chops with mixture.
2. Heat shortening in skillet and brown chops on both sides.
3. Place chops in cooker and add soup.
4. Cook on low 6-8 hours, or on high 3-4 hours.

Yield: 6-8 servings

PEACHY PORK CHOPS

Scalloped potatoes go well with these chops, as does a simple salad of chicory, escarole or endive.

4 pork chops, cut 1½ inches thick	1 tablespoon shortening
½ teaspoon allspice	1 teaspoon salt
½ teaspoon rosemary	½ cup peach nectar
1 tablespoon Dijon-style mustard	½ cup light cream
2 tablespoons brown sugar	1 can peach halves

1. Mix allspice and rosemary, rub pork chops with mixture, and let stand 1 hour.
2. Mix mustard and brown sugar together and coat chops.
3. Heat shortening in skillet and brown chops well.
4. Place chops in cooker, season with salt, and pour in nectar.
5. Cook on low 6-8 hours, or on high 3-4 hours.
6. Stir in cream and heat.
7. Serve garnished with peaches.

Yield: 4 servings

HERB-STUFFED CHOPS

6 double pork chops, with pockets cut by butcher
2 teaspoons salt
½ teaspoon pepper
3 tablespoons butter
¾ cup chopped onion
¼ cup chopped celery
1½ cups bread cubes
½ cup chopped parsley
1 teaspoon anise or fennel
1 small can evaporated milk
2 tablespoons shortening
¾ cup dry white wine

1. Rub chops inside and out with salt and pepper.
2. In a skillet heat butter and sauté onion and celery until onion is transparent. Remove from heat and add bread, parsley, anise and milk.
3. Stuff the pork chops with the bread mixture, closing with toothpicks.
4. Heat shortening in skillet and brown chops on both sides.
5. Place chops in cooker and add wine.
6. Cook on low 8-9 hours, or on high 4-5 hours.

Yield: 6 servings

PORK CHOPS WITH KNOCKWURST

6 shoulder pork chops,
cut about ¾ inch
thick
½ cup flour
1½ teaspoons salt
¼ teaspoon pepper
3 tablespoons shorten-
ing
3 medium onions,
chopped
1 carrot, thinly sliced

1 stalk celery and top,
chopped
6 medium potatoes,
thinly sliced
1 1-pound can toma-
toes, drained and
chopped
1 pound knockwurst,
cut in ¼-inch slices
1 cup chicken stock

1. Mix flour, salt and pepper and dredge chops with
   mixture.
2. Heat shortening in skillet and brown chops on
   both sides.
3. Place meat and all other ingredients in cooker.
4. Cook on low 6-8 hours, on high 3-4 hours, or on
   automatic 5 hours.

Yield: 6 servings

SAUCY PORK CASSEROLE

2 pounds boneless
pork, cut into 1½-
inch pieces
2 tablespoons soy sauce
2 tablespoons shorten-
ing
2 medium onions,
thinly sliced

1 8-ounce can tomato
sauce
1½ teaspoons sugar
¼ teaspoon pepper
2 tablespoons prepared
horseradish
¼ teaspoon nutmeg

1. Coat pork pieces with 2 tablespoons soy sauce.
2. Heat shortening in skillet. Sauté pork and pour
   off fat.
3. Place meat in cooker. Add sliced onions.
4. In small bowl combine remaining ingredients and
   mix well. Pour into cooker.
5. Cook on low 10-12 hours, or on automatic 6-7
   hours.

Yield: 5-6 servings

PORK STEWED IN WINE

This Italian dish is known as *maiale affogato,* or "drowned pork." A close relative, made with Chianti, is *maiale ubriacato*—literally, "drunken pork." Try serving it with cold asparagus salad.

3 pounds boneless pork, cut into 1-inch cubes	1 1-pound can tomatoes, drained and chopped
2 tablespoons olive oil	1½ teaspoons salt
2 cloves garlic, crushed	½ teaspoon rosemary
3 medium carrots, sliced	¼ teaspoon pepper
3 green peppers, cut into 1-inch squares	1 cup dry white wine

1. Heat oil in skillet and sauté garlic. Add meat and brown lightly.
2. Place vegetables in cooker, add meat and seasonings, and pour in wine.
3. Cook on low 6-7 hours, on high 3-4 hours, or on automatic 5 hours.

Yield: 6-8 servings

ORIENTAL STEW

2 pounds boneless pork, cut into 1-inch cubes
1 onion, sliced
1 green pepper, cut in strips
1 cup sliced celery
1 5-ounce can water chestnuts, drained and sliced
1 4-ounce can sliced mushrooms
1 can mandarin orange segments
3 tablespoons soy sauce
1 teaspoon ginger

1. Combine all ingredients in cooker.
2. Cook on low 8-10 hours, or on automatic 4 hours.

Yield: 6-8 servings

BARBECUED RIBS

3 pounds spareribs
¼ teaspoon salt
¼ teaspoon pepper
1 large onion, sliced
1 clove garlic, minced
2 cups barbecue sauce

1. Put ribs in broiler pan and broil for about 25 minutes, or until browned. Discard fat.
2. Cut ribs into serving pieces, sprinkle with salt and pepper, and place in cooker. Add all other ingredients.
3. Cook on low 6-8 hours, or on high 3-4 hours.

Yield: 5-6 servings

CASSOULET

This well-known French dish, like many other stand-bys, can be made in several different ways. This version goes well with hard rolls and a salad of thinly sliced cucumbers.

2 cups dried white beans
1½ pounds boneless pork, cut into 1-inch cubes
1 pound boneless lamb, cut into 1-inch cubes
3 slices bacon, diced
1½ cups chopped onion
3 cloves garlic, minced
2 garlic sausages, sliced
1 tablespoon salt
4 cloves
2 bay leaves
1 teaspoon thyme
1 8-ounce can tomato sauce
1½ cups dry white wine

1. Soak beans overnight in water to cover. Drain.
2. In skillet, sauté bacon and remove. Brown pork and lamb in bacon fat.
3. Combine bacon, pork, lamb, and all other ingredients in cooker. If liquid is insufficient, add water to about half an inch below the level of the food.
4. Cook on low 10 hours.

Yield: 6-8 servings

SWEET AND SOUR PORK

1½ pounds boneless pork, cut into 2-inch strips
1 teaspoon paprika
2 tablespoons shortening
1 small onion, thinly sliced
1 green pepper, cut into strips
3 tablespoons brown sugar

4 tablespoons instant dry milk
2 tablespoons cornstarch
½ teaspoon salt
1 15½-ounce can pineapple tidbits, drained (reserve syrup)
⅓ cup vinegar
1 tablespoon soy sauce
1 tablespoon Worcestershire sauce

1. Sprinkle pork pieces with paprika.
2. Heat shortening in skillet. Sauté pork and discard fat.
3. Place meat in cooker. Add onion and pepper.
4. Combine next four ingredients in bowl. Then add vinegar, soy sauce, Worcestershire sauce, and ⅔ cup pineapple liquid (if juice does not make this much, add water). Pour entire mixture into cooker.
5. Cook on low 8-9 hours, or on high 4-5 hours. During last 1-2 hours, add pineapple.

Yield: 6 servings

BRAISED HAM

1 2-2½ pound smoked
  boneless pork shoulder
  butt
1 stalk celery, sliced
1 carrot, sliced

6 whole cloves
4 whole peppercorns
1 bay leaf
2 cups water

1. Combine all ingredients in cooker.
2. Cook on low 6-8 hours, or on high 3-4 hours.

Yield: 6 servings

SPARERIBS AND SAUERKRAUT

3 pounds spareribs
¼ teaspoon salt
⅛ teaspoon pepper
2 large onions, sliced

1 11-ounce can sauer-
  kraut
½ teaspoon caraway
  seeds
1 cup water

1. Put ribs in broiler pan and broil for about 25
   minutes, or until browned. Discard fat.
2. Cut ribs into serving pieces, and sprinkle with
   salt and pepper.
3. In cooker, alternate layers of ribs, onions and
   sauerkraut. Sprinkle with caraway seeds and add
   water.
4. Cook on low 7-8 hours, or on automatic 3-4 hours.

Yield: 5-6 servings

HAM IN WINE

1 slice of ham about
¾ inch thick (about
1 pound)
½ cup cider or apple
juice
¼ cup sweet red wine
¼ cup maple syrup
1 small package (1½
ounces) raisins

1 8-ounce can cran-
berries
1 8-ounce can sliced
pineapple, drained
whole cloves

1½ tablespoons flour or
cornstarch

1. Cut ham into serving pieces and place in cooker.
2. Combine next five ingredients in bowl.
3. Put a clove in each slice of pineapple and place
   on top of ham. Pour wine and fruit mixture into
   cooker.
4. Cook on low 2 hours, then switch to high 4 hours.
   Or cook on automatic 4-5 hours.
5. To thicken sauce, remove ¼ cup liquid from
   cooker, combine with flour, and return to pot.

Yield: 3-4 servings

SCALLOPED HAM AND POTATOES

6 serving slices ham, cut about ¼-inch thick

6-8 medium potatoes, thinly sliced

1 cup chopped onion

1½ teaspoons salt

¼ teaspoon pepper

1 cup grated Cheddar cheese

1 can cream of celery soup

⅛ teaspoon paprika

1. Alternate ingredients in cooker as follows: half the ham, potatoes, and onions; half the salt and pepper; half the grated cheese. Repeat with second layer.
2. Spread soup over food so air does not reach potatoes. Sprinkle with paprika.
3. Cook on low 8-9 hours, or on high 4-5 hours.

Yield: 6 servings

HAM HOCKS WITH VEGETABLES

3-4 pounds smoked ham
   hocks
  6 carrots, sliced
  6 medium potatoes,
   quartered
  6 small onions, halved

1 small cabbage, cut
  into chunks
2 cloves garlic, split
1 bay leaf
8 peppercorns
1½ cups water

mustard

1. Place all ingredients in cooker.
2. Cook on low 8 hours, on high 5 hours, or on automatic 3-4 hours.
3. Remove ham hocks from cooker, cut meat from bones, and return meat to pot. Skim off fat from top of cooker.
4. Serve with good hot mustard.

Yield: 6 servings

HINTS FOR THE COOK

● If you're preparing a roast in your slow cooker —whether beef, veal, lamb, or pork—you may want to test it for doneness by using a meat thermometer. Insert this in the meat just as you would if you were cooking in an oven. Remember to keep the point away from bones in the meat, and see that the top doesn't touch the lid of your cooker.

● While everybody knows about cooked spinach, some have never tried the vegetable raw in a salad. Its dark green color contrasts nicely with lighter leaf or head lettuce. If you grow your own, or can buy spinach in bulk (rather than packaged), concentrate on the smaller leaves. You'll find them more manageable to clean and eat.

Poultry

Versatile and inexpensive, poultry has won wide
popularity in recent years, especially since you can
now buy the parts you like best without having to
cope with those awkward necks, backs and gizzards.
A French king once promised his subjects "a
chicken in every pot"; try one in your slow cooker
and you'll see that they're eminently suited. Two
cautions: (1) Chicken doesn't take as long to cook
as most other meats. If you cook it with vegetables,
the meat may fall off the bones by the time the
vegetables are done. This makes for quite tasty
eating, but just watch out for small bones as you
dig in. (2) Duck has lots of fat just under the
skin, so you should provide for its removal. Brown
the meat in advance if you can, pricking the skin
with a fork occasionally.

ROAST CHICKEN IN A POT

1 3-4 pound chicken	1 teaspoon poultry
2 teaspoons salt	seasoning
¼ teaspoon pepper	¼ teaspoon basil
	(optional)

1. Sprinkle chicken cavity with salt, pepper and poultry seasoning.
2. Place chicken in cooker and sprinkle with basil.
3. Cook on low 8-10 hours, or on high 4-6 hours.

Yield: 4-5 servings

Note: Meat may be removed from bone and used for chicken salad, chicken tetrazzini or other recipes requiring cooked chicken.

COQ AU VIN

The French way of saying "chicken [actually a rooster] in wine." Serve it with small new potatoes dusted with parsley. Another good, though unorthodox, accompaniment would be hash-browned potatoes.

2 frying chickens, cut up	¼ teaspoon pepper
12-16 small whole onions	1 cup chicken stock
½ pound mushrooms, sliced	1 cup dry white or red wine
1 teaspoon salt	3 tablespoons flour
½ teaspoon thyme	3 tablespoons butter

1. Place onions in bottom of cooker, then add all other ingredients except butter and flour.
2. Cook on low 8-10 hours, or on high 3-4 hours.
3. To thicken sauce, remove ¼ cup liquid from cooker. Melt butter in saucepan, stir in flour, and add liquid. When thoroughly blended, return to cooker.

Yield: 6-8 servings

CHICKEN IN SOUR CREAM

3 large chicken breasts,
  split
1½ teaspoons salt
¼ teaspoon pepper
¼ teaspoon paprika
½ cup dry white wine

1 can condensed
  cream of mushroom
  soup
½ pound mushrooms,
  sliced

1 cup sour cream

1. Rub chicken well with seasonings. Place in cooker.
2. Mix next three ingredients together and pour over chicken.
3. Cook on low 6-8 hours, or on high 2-3 hours.
4. Remove chicken from cooker. Stir in sour cream and heat through. Return chicken to pot.

Yield: 6 servings

BARBECUED CHICKEN WINGS

5 pounds chicken wings, with tips cut off
1 12-ounce bottle chili sauce
⅓ cup lemon juice
1 tablespoon Worcestershire sauce
2 tablespoons molasses
2 teaspoons salt
2 teaspoons chili powder
¼ teaspoon hot pepper sauce
dash garlic salt

1. Place wings in cooker.
2. Combine all remaining ingredients and pour over chicken.
3. Cook on low 6-8 hours, or on high 2-3 hours.

Yield: 6-8 servings

Note: Tips cut from chicken wings can be used for soup if you wish.

DRUMSTICKS MEXICAN

A tasty change from ordinary chicken combinations.
Delicious served with cornbread and cucumber sticks.

6 drumsticks with
 thighs, disjointed
1 teaspoon salt
¼ teaspoon pepper
1 cup thinly sliced
 celery

2 12-ounce cans
 Mexican-style corn

2 packages frozen lima
 beans, thawed

6 slices bacon

1. Sprinkle chicken with salt and pepper. Place in cooker.
2. Add celery and canned corn.
3. Cook on low 6-7 hours, or on high 2-3 hours.
4. Add lima beans and cook 1 hour longer.
5. Sauté bacon and crumble over top of casserole.

Yield: 6 servings

CHICKEN AND MUSHROOMS IN BEER

A subtle combination of flavors, and a good match for some crispy potatoes—French fries or hash browns.

2½ pounds chicken pieces	2 garlic cloves, minced
1 tablespoon salt	1½ cups sliced mushrooms
¼ teaspoon pepper	½ teaspoon marjoram
½ cup chopped scallions	½ teaspoon tarragon
	1 can beer

1. Place chicken in cooker and season with salt and pepper.
2. Add all other ingredients to cooker.
3. Cook on low 6-7 hours.

Yield: 5-6 servings

CHICKEN CACCIATORE

Many countries have some form of hunter's stew; this one is from Italy. Garlic bread and a green salad sprinkled with Parmesan or Romano cheese go well with it.

1 3-pound frying chicken, cut up	⅓ cup minced green pepper
3 tablespoons shortening	1 teaspoon salt
	1 teaspoon oregano
2 medium onions, thinly sliced	½ teaspoon basil
	½ teaspoon celery salt
2 cloves garlic, minced	¼ teaspoon pepper
1 1-pound can tomatoes	¼ teaspoon cayenne
1 8-ounce can tomato sauce	1 bay leaf, crumbled
	¼ cup dry red wine

1. Heat shortening in skillet and brown chicken pieces.
2. Place chicken in cooker, cover with onion slices, then add all other ingredients.
3. Cook on low 6-8 hours, or on high 3-4 hours.

Yield: 4-6 servings

NEAPOLITAN CHICKEN

Another one-pot meal. If you want to maintain the Italian mood, serve it with breadsticks or hot garlic bread.

4 pounds chicken pieces	¼ cup chopped parsley
1 medium onion, chopped	1 clove garlic, minced
	1 teaspoon salt
4 medium potatoes, cut in 1-inch cubes	⅛ teaspoon pepper
	½ teaspoon basil
1 large green pepper, cut in strips	1 1-pound jar spaghetti sauce

1. Combine all ingredients in cooker.
2. Cook on low 6-8 hours, or on high 3-4 hours.

Yield: 6-8 servings

SHERRY-OLIVE CHICKEN

Sherry and black olives give this chicken casserole a Spanish flavor, but actually it's of Mexican origin. It's good with brown rice and a dilled-cucumber salad.

1 3½-pound chicken,
 cut up
2 cloves garlic, minced
2 medium onions,
 chopped
1 bay leaf, crumbled
1 tablespoon chili
 powder

1 teaspoon oregano
2 4½-ounce cans
 pitted ripe olives,
 sliced
1½ teaspoons salt
1 cup water
½ cup sherry

1. Combine all ingredients in cooker.
2. Cook on low 6-8 hours, or on high 3-4 hours.

Yield: 4-6 servings

CHICKEN TETRAZZINI

In spite of its name, this concoction originated not in Italy but in the United States—probably in San Francisco. It was, however, named after an Italian, the turn-of-the-century coloratura Luisa Tetrazzini, whose ample girth attested to her love of pasta.

3 cups diced cooked
    chicken
2 cups chicken stock
½ cup finely chopped
    onion
½ cup white wine
½ pound mushrooms,
    sliced

1 can condensed cream
    of mushroom soup

8 ounces spaghetti,
    cooked
grated Parmesan
    cheese

1. Combine all ingredients except spaghetti and cheese in cooker. Stir well.
2. Cook on high 1 hour, then switch to low 6-8 hours. Or cook on automatic 7 hours.
3. Serve over spaghetti and sprinkle with cheese.

Yield: 5-6 servings

CHICKEN MARENGO

This is a much simplified version of an entrée created for Napoleon after his victory over the Austrian army at Marengo in 1800. According to the story, his chef had soldiers scurrying about the countryside of northern Italy looking for ingredients. Thus the dish as classically served is garnished with eggs and sliced French bread, both deep-fried in olive oil, plus anchovies and cooked crayfish. This may be a case where lack of all the original fixings improves the result.

2 fryers, cut up
12-16 small white onions
1 pound mushrooms
4 shallots, chopped
  (if not available,
  use white end of
  scallions)
2 cloves garlic,
  minced
1½ teaspoons salt
¼ teaspoon pepper

2 teaspoons thyme
5 sprigs parsley
2 bay leaves,
  crumbled
½ cup stuffed olives,
  sliced
1 1-pound can
  tomatoes
½ cup dry white wine

croutons

1. Place onions in bottom of cooker; add chicken and sliced mushrooms.
2. In bowl, mix all other ingredients except croutons and add to cooker.
3. Cook on low 6-8 hours, on high 3-4 hours, or on automatic 5 hours.
4. Serve with croutons.

Yield: 8 servings

CHICKEN CREOLE

3 pounds chicken
pieces
1 medium onion, sliced
1 medium green
pepper, cut into thin
strips
½ cup diced celery
1½ teaspoons salt
1 teaspoon thyme

½ teaspoon paprika
2 tablespoons chopped
parsley
1 1-pound can
tomatoes
1 4-ounce can sliced
mushrooms, drained
(optional)

1. Combine all ingredients in cooker.
2. Cook on high 4-5 hours.

Yield: 4-6 servings

CURRIED CHICKEN

Serve over rice. And have on hand at least some of the traditional curry garnishes: raisins, grated coconut, peanuts, slivered almonds or chutney.

4 pounds chicken pieces	1½ tablespoons curry powder
1 large onion, chopped	1 teaspoon ginger
1 large apple, quartered, pared, cored and chopped	½ teaspoon salt
	2 cups chicken stock
2 cloves garlic, minced	1 cup yogurt
	2 tablespoons flour

1. Place chicken, onion, apple and garlic in cooker.
2. Combine next four ingredients and pour into pot.
3. Cook on low 6-7 hours, or on high 3-4 hours.
4. Remove chicken and stir in yogurt. When well blended, remove ¼ cup sauce, blend with flour, and return to cooker. Return chicken to cooker.

Yield: 6 servings

ARROZ CON POLLO

Like beef stew, this basic dish varies from one Spanish-speaking country to another. Naturally, it always includes rice and chicken. A simple green salad and perhaps a custard dessert (*flan* is the Spanish variety) would complete your meal.

1 3-4 pound chicken, cut up
1 teaspoon salt
½ teaspoon pepper
1 teaspoon paprika
1 cup chopped onion
1 cup chopped green pepper
2 cloves garlic, minced
1 2-ounce jar pimiento, diced

1 3½-ounce jar stuffed green olives, drained and sliced
¾ teaspoon chili powder
2 bouillon cubes
1 cup diced ham
1 1-pound can tomatoes

1 cup raw rice
1 package frozen peas

1. Mix salt, pepper and paprika, and season chicken with mixture
2. Place chicken in cooker and cover with all other ingredients except rice and peas.
3. Cook on low 6-8 hours, or on high 4 hours.
4. Add rice and peas and cook 1 more hour on high, stirring occasionally.

Yield: 4-6 servings

BROWN RICE AND CHICKEN

1 cup diced cooked
chicken

2 onions, chopped

2 stalks celery, chopped

2 cups cooked brown
rice

¼ cup dry white wine

2 cups chicken broth

slivered almonds

1. Combine all ingredients in cooker.
2. Cook on low 6-8 hours, or on automatic 4-5 hours.
3. Serve with slivered almonds lightly browned in
   butter.

Yield: 4 servings

CHICKEN GREEK STYLE

Try serving this with sautéed eggplant slices and flat Syrian-style bread, if available.

1 fryer, cut up	3 tablespoons shortening
3 tablespoons flour	3 small onions, sliced thin
1 teaspoon salt	½ cup chicken broth
¼ teaspoon pepper	½ cup lemon juice
½ teaspoon oregano	

1. Mix flour and seasonings together and dredge chicken with mixture.
2. Heat shortening in skillet and brown chicken.
3. Place chicken in cooker and add other ingredients.
4. Cook on high 3-4 hours.

Yield: 4-5 servings

CHICKEN WITH LENTILS

You might serve this with a cranberry and orange molded salad, or sliced cranberry jelly. And add some brown-and-serve rolls to sop up the cooking juices.

1 pound lentils	1 3-pound fryer, cut up
1½ teaspoons salt	5 slices bacon, diced
2 cloves garlic, minced	water or chicken broth
1 bay leaf	

1. Soak lentils in water overnight.
2. Place lentils, with water, in cooker. Add salt, garlic, and bay leaf.
3. Cook 4-6 hours on high.
4. Add chicken and bacon to cooker. If more liquid is necessary, add water or broth.
5. Cook on low 4-5 hours, or on high 3 hours.

Yield: 5-6 servings

DUCK WITH KIDNEY BEANS

1 pound kidney beans
1 4-4½ pound duck,
  quartered
1 pound hot Italian
  sausage
1 pound sweet Italian
  sausage
1 onion, thinly sliced

1½ teaspoons salt
¼ teaspoon pepper
½ teaspoon dry mustard
¼ teaspoon basil
½ teaspoon anise or
  fennel seed
  (optional)

1. Soak beans overnight.
2. Preheat oven to 450°. Brown duck (pricking skin to release fat) and sausages for 30 minutes. Discard fat.
3. Combine all ingredients in cooker.
4. Cook on low 7-8 hours, or on automatic 3-4 hours.

Yield: 4-6 servings

DUCK CALCUTTA

1 4-5 pound duck, cut up

2 tablespoons shortening

2 large onions, sliced

1 medium orange, peeled and diced

3 cups sauerkraut, undrained (use fresh if available)

2 cloves garlic, crushed

½ cup firmly packed brown sugar

⅓ cup flour

2 tablespoons curry powder

1 teaspoon ginger

½ teaspoon tarragon

½ teaspoon marjoram

½ bay leaf, crumbled

2 teaspoons salt

½ teaspoon pepper

1 cup chicken stock

1. Heat shortening in skillet. Brown duck well and discard fat.
2. Place onion and orange in bottom of cooker. Add duck.
3. Mix all other ingredients together and pour into cooker.
4. Cook on high 3 hours, then switch to low 3-4 hours. Or cook on automatic 5 hours.

Yield: 6 servings

DUCK WITH APPLESAUCE

1 5-pound duck, cut up
2 tablespoons shortening
2 teaspoons salt
½ teaspoon pepper

½ cup chopped parsley
1 1-pound can applesauce
1 onion, chopped

1. Heat shortening in skillet. Brown duck well and discard fat.
2. Mix salt, pepper, parsley and applesauce.
3. Place half of applesauce mixture in bottom of cooker, add duck and onion, then cover with remaining applesauce mixture.
4. Cook on high 3 hours, then switch to low 4 hours. Or cook on automatic for 5-6 hours.

Yield: 5 servings

Note: If cooked duck produces much fat, skim off top of cooker. Or you may wish to refrigerate in a casserole overnight and remove fat when duck has chilled.

TURKEY-OLIVE CASSEROLE

5-6 pounds turkey parts
   (if not available, use
   chicken)
3 tablespoons flour
2 teaspoons salt
¼ teaspoon pepper
3 tablespoons shorten-
   ing

½ pound bacon, diced
½ cup chopped shallots
   or scallions
1 1-pound can tomatoes
   drained
1 cup pitted ripe olives,
   sliced

1. Mix flour, salt and pepper together and dredge turkey with mixture.
2. Heat shortening in skillet. Brown turkey well and discard fat.
3. Place turkey in cooker and add all other ingredients.
4. Cook on low 6-7 hours.

Yield: 8 servings

Fish

There's no escaping the fact that most fish is best when cooked quickly, being delicate and light in texture. But a slow cooker is good for mixtures (such as seafood Naples), for salmon and tuna casseroles (such as tuna Niçoise), and for sauces to which you add shellfish at the last minute (creole jambalaya). And, for variety, don't forget fish chowder (see under "Soups").

MACARONI-SHRIMP CURRY

This is an unusual all-in-one curry. Try it with a salad of lettuce and avocado, and hot rolls.

1 pound cooked, cleaned shrimp, cut into pieces if desired
1 cup chopped onions
½ cup sliced celery
1 cup chopped apple
½ cup shredded coconut
½ cup chopped walnuts
1 teaspoon salt
¼ teaspoon pepper
1 tablespoon curry powder
¼ teaspoon ginger
2 cans condensed cream of celery soup
½ cup water
1 8-ounce package elbow macaroni, cooked

1. Combine all ingredients except macaroni in cooker and stir.
2. Cook on low 6-8 hours, or on high 4 hours.
3. Add cooked macaroni and heat.

Yield: 6 servings

SALMON LOAF

1 1-pound can salmon,
with liquid
1 4½-ounce jar mush-
rooms, drained
1½ cups bread crumbs
2 eggs, beaten

1 cup grated Cheddar
cheese
1 tablespoon lemon
juice
1 tablespoon minced
onion

1. Flake fish in bowl to remove all skin and bones.
2. Combine all ingredients in bowl and mix well.
3. Place salmon mixture in well-greased cooker.
4. Cook on high 1 hour, then switch to low 3-4 hours.

Yield: 3-4 servings

TUNAFISH CASSEROLE

1 7-ounce can tuna
4 slices bread, cubed
1 can condensed cream
of mushroom soup
1½ cups grated Cheddar
cheese
3 eggs, beaten

½ cup stuffed green
olives, sliced
¾ teaspoon salt
1 teaspoon Wor-
cestershire sauce
1 cup dry white wine

1. Combine all ingredients in bowl and mix well.
2. Place tuna mixture in well-greased cooker.
3. Cook on low 3-4 hours, or on high 1-2 hours.

Yield: 4 servings

SEAFOOD NAPLES

1 5-ounce can shrimp,
  drained
1 13-ounce can tuna
1 6½-ounce can crab
  meat, drained and
  cartilage removed
1 4-ounce can
  pimiento. drained
  and diced
¼ cup chopped parsley

1½ cups instant rice,
  uncooked
1 can condensed cream
  of mushroom soup
1 cup water
½ cup dry white wine
2 teaspoons instant
  onion flakes
1 teaspoon dill weed
¼ teaspoon paprika
¼ teaspoon Tabasco

1. Place first six ingredients in cooker.
2. Combine soup with next six ingredients. Pour into cooker and stir well.
3. Cook on low 2-3 hours.

Yield: 6 servings

BAKED TUNA NICOISE

This is a cooked version of the famous *salade Niçoise*, a specialty of the region around Nice. Serve with French or Italian bread.

2 7-ounce cans tuna	⅓ cup chopped parsley
3 small new potatoes, diced	1 8-ounce can tomato sauce
3 scallions, chopped	
2 2-ounce jars pimiento, chopped	1 package frozen green beans, cooked
6-8 pitted black olives, sliced	
1 teaspoon salt	1 tablespoon capers
⅛ teaspoon pepper	4-6 anchovies, cut in pieces

1. Combine first nine ingredients in cooker.
2. Cook on low 4-5 hours, or on automatic 2½ hours.
3. Add beans and heat through.
4. Garnish with capers and anchovies.

Yield: 4-5 servings

EASY FISH FILLETS

1 pound frozen fish
fillets—mackerel,
flounder or sole
2 onions, chopped
1 green pepper, cut into
thin strips
1 4½-ounce jar mush-
rooms, drained

1 teaspoon salt
½ teaspoon paprika
1 clove garlic, crushed
½ cup lemon juice
1 1-pound can tomatoes
in purée

lemon slices
chopped parsley

1. Combine all ingredients except lemon and parsley
   in cooker.
2. Cook 6-7 hours on automatic.
3. Garnish with lemon and parsley.

Yield: 4 servings

CREOLE JAMBALAYA

The Creole cooking of New Orleans and its surroundings is a spicy wedding of French Louisiana styles and innovations introduced by the black population. ("Jambalaya," for instance, is a form of the French word *jambon,* meaning "ham.") Rice is a must to complete this meal, and you might have a rich chocolate concoction for dessert.

1 pound ham, cut into
   1-inch cubes
1 large green pepper,
   chopped
1 large onion, chopped
1 clove garlic, minced
1 28-ounce can
   tomatoes, drained and
   chopped
¼ cup minced parsley

1 teaspoon salt
1 tablespoon Worcestershire sauce
½ teaspoon thyme
¼ teaspoon cayenne or
   ⅛ teaspoon Tabasco
   sauce

1 pound frozen cleaned
   shrimp, thawed

1. Combine all ingredients except shrimp in cooker.
2. Cook on low 5-6 hours.
3. Add shrimp and cook 1 hour on high.

Yield: 6 servings

HINTS FOR THE COOK

• If you do much cooking, sooner or later you'll find yourself with leftover egg whites or yolks. What to do? Buy an inexpensive ice cube tray—the kind with a separate, detachable plastic container for each cube. Use each container to hold a single white or yolk. After they freeze solid, they can be stacked on top of each other. They're easy to keep track of, and to thaw.

• The next time you prepare a hot punch, try making it in your electric slow cooker. Use a favorite recipe for hot buttered rum, mulled wine or spiced fruit juice. Combine the ingredients in the cooker, and cook on high for 1 or 2 hours. Then you can switch to low and keep the punch warm for as long as you like. Serve it directly from the cooker.

Vegetable Dishes

Among the very first slow cookers in America were bean pots, into which colonial housekeepers stirred tasty mixtures of beans, molasses and meat to simmer for many hours. Electric slow cookers do well by beans, which require long, slow cooking. If soaking dried beans overnight (plus pot-cooking with other ingredients) seems to take too long, try parboiling them. Boil them in a saucepan about 15-20 minutes and let them stand in the water for an hour; or place them in your slow cooker and cook on high for 2-3 hours. In either case, add the other ingredients and cook until done. Vegetarians favor bean dishes because they're high in protein. Try the pinto beans with chutney, or Mexican limas (without the bacon garnish). And then experiment with some of your own favorite meatless meals.

BAKED NAVY BEANS

3 cups navy beans
9 cups water
3 teaspoons salt
½ cup chopped onion
½ pound salt pork, cut
  into 1-inch cubes

¼ cup molasses
1 cup ketchup
¼ cup firmly packed
  brown sugar
2 teaspoons dry mustard

1. Wash and pick over beans. Place in cooker.
2. Add water, salt, onion and pork. Mix well so beans cover pork.
3. Cook on low 13-15 hours, or until beans are tender.
4. Drain beans, reserving liquid. Add last four ingredients to cooker and stir. Return 2 cups bean liquid and blend well.
5. Cook on low 3-4 hours.

Yield: 8-10 servings

Note: Cooking time can be reduced if beans are soaked overnight before cooking. If you do this, cook on low 8-10 hours.

HONEY-BAKED BLACK-EYED PEAS

2 cups black-eyed peas
6 slices bacon, diced
1 medium onion,
minced
1 teaspoon salt
⅛ teaspoon pepper

1 teaspoon dry mustard
2 tablespoons chopped
preserved ginger (or 1
teaspoon powdered)
¾ cup honey

1. Cover peas with water and cook on low overnight.
2. Fry bacon until crisp; discard fat.
3. Combine all ingredients in cooker.
4. Cook on low 8-9 hours.

Yield: 4 servings

SPICY LIMA BEANS

1 pound dried lima
beans

1 hambone or ham
hock

½ cup firmly packed
dark brown sugar

2 tablespoons minced
onions

½ teaspoon ground
cloves

½ teaspoon dry
mustard

1½ teaspoons salt

1. Wash and pick over beans. Place in cooker and
   add water to 1 inch above beans.
2. Cook beans overnight on low.
3. Drain beans, reserving liquid.
4. In bowl, combine sugar and next four ingredients
   with 2 cups bean liquid. (Add water if cooking
   liquid is less than 2 cups.)
5. Place beans and ham in cooker and add brown
   sugar mixture.
6. Cook on low 9-10 hours.

Yield: 8 servings

PINTO BEANS WITH CHUTNEY

1 pound pinto beans	1 teaspoon salt
1 onion, chopped	¼ teaspoon pepper
½ cup chutney, minced	½ cup honey
1½ teaspoons dry mustard	½ cup yogurt

1. Wash beans and place in cooker. Add enough water to cover.
2. Cook on high 2 hours.
3. Add all other ingredients to cooker.
4. Cook on low 8 hours.

Yield: 4-6 servings

SLOW-COOKER SOYBEANS

1½ cups soybeans	½ teaspoon salt
1 ham hock or hambone	¼ teaspoon pepper
1 small onion, chopped	½ teaspoon dry mustard
½ cup ketchup	1 teaspoon Worcestershire sauce
2 tablespoons molasses	

1. Soak beans overnight in water (using about 4½ cups).
2. Place beans in cooker in soaking water. Cook on high for 3 hours.
3. Add other ingredients to cooker.
4. Cook on low 12-14 hours, or until tender.

Yield: 4-6 servings

KIDNEY BEANS WITH CHEESE

6 slices bacon, diced
2 cans kidney beans,
  drained
1 onion, chopped
1 clove garlic, minced
2 tablespoons chili
  powder

1 teaspoon salt
½ teaspoon rosemary
1 8-ounce can tomato
  sauce
2 cups Cheddar or
  Monterey Jack cheese,
  diced

1. Fry bacon until crisp; discard fat.
2. Combine all ingredients except cheese in cooker.
   Add cheese on top.
3. Cook on automatic 1-2 hours.

Yield: 6 servings

BEAN-SAUSAGE CASSEROLE

3 1-pound cans kidney
   beans, drained
6 strips bacon, diced
2 kielbasa sausages (if
   not available, use
   knockwurst)

1 cup chopped onion
1½ teaspoons salt
¼ teaspoon pepper
1½ cups red wine

chopped parsley

1. Fry bacon bits until crisp discard fat.
2. Combine all ingredients except parsley in cooker.
3. Cook on low 8-10 hours, on high 5 hours, or on automatic 6 hours.
4. Garnish with parsley.

Yield: 6-8 servings

LIMA-HAM DINNER

1 pound dried lima
  beans
½ pound ham, diced
1 cup chopped onion
1 large green pepper,
  chopped

1 teaspoon dry mustard
1 teaspoon salt
½ teaspoon pepper
1 can condensed cream
  of tomato soup
1 cup water

1. Soak beans overnight in water to cover. Drain.
2. Combine all ingredients in cooker.
3. Cook on low 8-10 hours, or on high 4-5 hours.

Yield: 4-6 servings

WHITE BEANS AND HAM

1 pound white beans—
navy, Great Northern
or pea beans
1 onion stuck with 2
cloves

1 piece ham shank or
hambone
1 stalk celery, sliced
1 bay leaf

1. Soak beans overnight in water to cover. Drain.
2. Combine all ingredients in cooker. Add water to cover.
3. Cook on low 9-10 hours, or until beans are tender.

Yield: 4-5 servings

LENTILS WITH SAUSAGE

2 cups lentils
8 Italian sausages,
either hot or sweet
(or half and half)
1 large onion, chopped

1 bay leaf, crumbled
1½ teaspoons salt
¼ teaspoon pepper
½ cup red wine
beef stock

1. In water to cover, parboil sausage 10 minutes.
2. Combine all ingredients in cooker, adding enough stock to cover them.
3. Cook on low 8-10 hours, or on high 5-6 hours.

Yield: 6 servings

SAUERKRAUT AND SAUSAGE

In spite of its name, sauerkraut apparently originated in China, sometime in the 3rd century B.C. It was later recognized as a preventive against scurvy, and Captain James Cook—"discoverer" of Hawaii—took thousands of pounds on board his ships to protect his sailors against the disease.

3 strips bacon, diced	3 tablespoons dark brown sugar
1½ tablespoons flour	
2 27-ounce cans sauer-kraut	1½ teaspoons caraway seeds
2 small apples, peeled and cubed	2 kielbasa sausages, sliced thin
	½ cup water

1. Fry bacon bits until crisp; set aside.
2. Add flour to bacon fat and blend well; stir in sauerkraut.
3. Place sauerkraut and bacon in cooker. Add all other ingredients and mix well.
4. Cook on low 5-6 hours, or on high 3-4 hours.

Yield: 6 servings

MEXICAN LIMAS

1 pound dried lima
  beans
½ cup minced onion
1 green pepper, cut
  into strips
1 clove garlic, minced
1½ teaspoons salt

1 tablespoon dill weed
1 1-pound can
  tomatoes
1 4-ounce can tomato
  sauce

6 strips bacon, cooked

1. Soak beans overnight in water.
2. Drain beans. Place in cooker with all other ingredients except bacon.
3. Cook on high 3 hours, then switch to low 6 hours. Or cook on automatic 5-6 hours.
4. Garnish with crisp bacon.

Yield: 6 servings

HINTS FOR THE COOK

• The variety of dried beans is remarkable, and they're useful to have around because they keep so long. For instance, kidney beans come in both light and dark red shades, and there's a pink bean, too, which is equally good in Mexican-style cooking. If you have trouble finding certain types of beans in your supermarket, try a store that specializes in health foods.

• If you want just a whisper of garlic flavor, don't bother to mince a clove, Just peel it and stick a toothpick through it. Bury it in the food in your slow cooker. The toothpick makes it easy to retrieve, so you can remove it before serving your meal.

Accompaniments

One of the first questions people ask about slow cookers is, "Don't vegetables fall apart when they're cooked so long?" Oddly enough, they don't. The low temperatures keep them intact, and cooking liquids (which many vegetables, such as onions and tomatoes, produce in quantity) preserve nutrients that often get lost in top-of-the-stove cookery. Slow cooking is especially efficacious for dense but savory vegetables such as artichokes and cabbage. And if you want to preserve as much of the color as possible, cook vegetables on the high or the automatic setting of your cooker.

DILLED STEWED ARTICHOKES

This three-vegetable concoction has many possibilities. You can serve it all together to accompany a meat or fish main course. Or you can serve the artichokes alone as a side dish, reserving the onions and carrots for another meal. Or, vice versa—eat the other vegetables and chill the artichokes, having them (with a vinaigrette sauce) as a first course some other time.

4 artichokes (or 6-8 tiny ones, if available)	1½ teaspoons salt
	⅛ teaspoon pepper
1 lemon, cut in two	3 tablespoons fresh dill weed, chopped, or 1 tablespoon dried
16 small white onions	
4 large carrots, sliced	3 cups chicken stock

1. Cut off artichoke stalks and remove tough outer leaves. Wash artichokes and rub with cut lemon.
2. Place artichokes in cooker, filling spaces around them with onions and carrots. Sprinkle them with seasonings and pour in stock.
3. Cook on high 5 hours, or on automatic 6 hours.

Yield: 4-6 servings

ARTICHOKES

4-6 artichokes
1½ teaspoons salt
8 peppercorns

2 stalks celery, cut in
  2-3 pieces
½ lemon, sliced
2 cups boiling water

1. Cut off artichoke stalks and remove tough outer leaves. Wash thoroughly.
2. Place artichokes in cooker and add all other ingredients.
3. Cook on high 4-5 hours, or on automatic 6 hours.

Yield: 4-6 servings

BLACK BEANS AND RUM

A good side dish with roast poultry or game.

1 pound black beans	½ teaspoon thyme
1 ham hock or ham-bone	½ teaspoon savory
	1 cup water
1 small onion stuck with 2 cloves	
	2 tablespoons flour
1 garlic clove, minced	¼ cup rum
1 sprig parsley, chopped	½ teaspoon Tabasco sauce
1 bay leaf	
1½ teaspoons salt	sour cream

1. Soak beans overnight. Drain.
2. Place beans in cooker and add next nine ingredients.
3. Cook on high 3 hours, then switch to low 9 hours. Or cook on automatic 8 hours.
4. Remove ham and bay leaf. Cut meat off bone; return to pot.
5. In bowl, combine flour, rum and Tabasco sauce. Stir into cooker and blend well.
6. Serve with sour cream.

Yield: 6 servings

BOURBON-BRAISED ONIONS

These go well with steak, roasts or game. As you might guess, the recipe is Southern.

4 large onions, cut in ¼-inch slices	½ teaspoon pepper
1 teaspoon salt	¼ cup bouillon
	¼ cup Bourbon whiskey

1. Combine all ingredients in cooker.
2. Cook on high 5-6 hours.

Yield: 6 servings

GREEN BEAN CASSEROLE

1 1-pound can cut
   green beans, drained
1 3½-ounce can
   French-fried onion
   rings, crumbled
1 cup grated Cheddar
   cheese
1 8-ounce can water
   chestnuts

1 can condensed
   cream of chicken
   soup
¼ cup white wine
1½ teaspoons salt
½ teaspoon curry
   powder
¼ teaspoon pepper

1. In cooker, alternate layers as follows: beans, onion rings, cheese and water chestnuts.
2. Combine all other ingredients and add to cooker.
3. Cook on low 6-7 hours, or on high 3-4 hours. Or cook on automatic 5 hours.

Yield: 4-5 servings

GREEN BEANS AND TOMATOES

1½-2 pounds green
   beans
1 ham hock
1 small onion,
   chopped
1 teaspoon salt

⅛ teaspoon pepper
1 1-pound can toma-
   toes (with liquid),
   chopped
½ cup water

1. Wash beans, snip off ends, and cut or break into pieces about 2 inches long.
2. Combine all ingredients in cooker.
3. Cook on high 5 hours, or until tender.

Yield: 6-8 servings

BRAISED RED CABBAGE

1 medium red cabbage, shredded	3 tablespoons soy sauce
1 tablespoon salt	1½ tablespoons sugar
½ teaspoon pepper	1 bay leaf, crumbled
1 cup dry red wine	¼ teaspoon ginger
1 tablespoon wine vinegar	

1. Place cabbage in cooker; sprinkle with salt and pepper.
2. In bowl, combine all other ingredients, stir well, and pour into cooker.
3. Cook on high 4-5 hours, or on automatic 6 hours.

Yield: 6 servings

SWEET-SOUR CABBAGE

1 medium red or green cabbage, shredded	¼ cup lemon juice
2 onions, chopped	¼ cup cider or apple juice
4 tart apples, quartered, pared, cored, and chopped	3 tablespoons honey
	1 tablespoon caraway seeds
½ cup raisins	⅛ teaspoon allspice

1. Combine all ingredients in cooker.
2. Cook on high 5 hours, or on automatic 6 hours.

Yield: 6 servings

STEAMED ASPARAGUS

A slow cooker is ideal for asparagus, since even quite long stalks will fit into it well. Serve with butter or margarine. Or chill and serve with vinaigrette sauce.

2-3 pounds asparagus
1 teaspoon salt

¼ teaspoon lemon-
    pepper seasoning
½ cup boiling water

1. Wash asparagus well and snap off the lower ends of the stalks.
2. Place asparagus in cooker and add other ingredients.
3. Cook on high 2 hours, or until tender.

Yield: 4 servings

CARROTS IN WINE

6 large carrots, cut into sticks 2-3 inches long (if you can get baby carrots, use 12-15 whole ones)

4 scallions, chopped (include some of the green tops for extra flavor)

3 tablespoons chopped parsley
1 teaspoon salt
½ teaspoon thyme
½ teaspoon oregano
½ teaspoon sugar
¼ teaspoon pepper
½ cup chicken stock
½ cup dry white wine

chopped parsley

1. Place carrots and scallions in cooker.
2. In bowl, mix together all other ingredients except parsley garnish and pour into cooker.
3. Cook on high 2-3 hours, or until tender.
4. Garnish with chopped parsley.

Yield: 4-5 servings

BRAISED SAUERKRAUT

5 cups sauerkraut, drained (use fresh if available)

½ pound bacon (thick-cut if possible), diced

1 cup sliced onions

½ cup thinly sliced carrots

* bouquet garni consisting of 4 sprigs parsley, 6 peppercorns and 1 bay leaf

¼ cup gin

½ cup dry white wine

2 cups beef or chicken stock

1. Fry bacon until crisp; discard fat.
2. Combine all ingredients in cooker.
3. Cook on low 8 hours.

Yield: 6-8 servings

* *See pages 33–34.*

SAUERKRAUT WITH APPLES

3 slices bacon, diced
1 onion, chopped
4 cups sauerkraut,
   drained (use fresh if
   available)
2 apples, quartered,
   pared, cored and diced

1 teaspoon salt
¼ teaspoon pepper
1 can beer
½ teaspoon crushed
   juniper berries
   (optional)

1. In skillet sauté bacon lightly. Add onion and cook until soft.
2. Combine sauerkraut and next five ingredients in cooker. Add bacon and onion (with bacon drippings).
3. Cook on low 4-5 hours.

Yield: 6-8 servings

ACORN SQUASH

This goes well with roast pork, or with a slice of broiled ham.

3 acorn squash, cut in
  half and seeds
  scooped out
2 teaspoons salt
½ teaspoon pepper

6 tablespoons butter
2 tablespoons brown
  sugar
3 slices bacon, diced
½ cup water

1. Season six squash halves with salt and pepper. Sprinkle with other ingredients except water.
2. Pour water into cooker. Add squash, alternating rows so that halves do not rest directly over each other.
3. Cook on high 1 hour, then switch to low 5-6 hours. Or cook on automatic 4-5 hours.

Yield: 6 servings

SPINACH CASSEROLE

2 packages frozen
  chopped spinach,
  thawed
2 cups medium noodles
½ cup chopped onion
1 cup gated Cheddar or
  Swiss cheese

¼ cup butter or mar-
  garine
⅛ teaspoon nutmeg
1 can condensed cream
  of mushroom soup

1. Cook noodles until just slightly tender; drain.
2. Combine all ingredients in cooker.
3. Cook on high 1 hour, then switch to low 4-5 hours.
   Or cook on automatic 3-4 hours.

Yield: 8 servings

ZUCCHINI CASSEROLE

1 red onion, sliced
1 green pepper, cut in thin strips
4 medium zucchini (scrubbed but not peeled), sliced
1 10-ounce can tomatoes

1 cup chopped parsley
1 teaspoon salt
½ teaspoon pepper
½ teaspoon basil

1 tablespoon butter or margarine
¼ cup Parmesan grated cheese

1. Combine all ingredients in cooker except butter and cheese.
2. Cook on high 2 hours, or on automatic 3 hours.
3. Dot with butter and sprinkle with cheese. Cook 1½ hours more on low.

Yield: 4-6 servings

ITALIAN VEGETABLE STEW

4 medium potatoes,
   sliced lengthwise
5-6 small zucchini
   (scrubbed but not
   peeled), sliced
   lengthwise
1 large green pepper,
   cut in thin strips

1 large onion, chopped
1 cup chicken stock
1 clove garlic, minced
2 bay leaves, crumbled
1½ teaspoons salt
¼ teaspoon pepper
1 teaspoon oregano

1. Combine all ingredients in cooker.
2. Cook on high 2-3 hours, or on automatic 3-4 hours.

Yield: 4-5 servings

GREEK MIXED VEGETABLES

Try this mixture with roast beef, lamb or pork. *Briani* (the Greek name) can be made with other vegetables as substitutes. You might try fresh or frozen green beans, wax beans or yellow squash.

1 pound potatoes, sliced
2 large carrots, sliced
1½ pounds zucchini (scrubbed but not peeled), sliced
2 medium onions, sliced
2 pounds fresh or frozen okra

1 28-ounce can tomatoes, drained and chopped
2 cloves garlic, minced
2 teaspoons salt
¼ teaspoon pepper
1½ teaspoons oregano
½ cup chopped parsley
½ cup olive oil

1. In bowl, combine tomatoes and next six ingredients.
2. In cooker, arrange a layer of potatoes, carrots, zucchini, onions and okra; sprinkle with some tomato mixture. Continue until vegetables are used up, ending with tomato mixture.
3. Cook on low 6-8 hours, on high 4-6 hours, or on automatic 5 hours.

Yield: 6-8 servings

BARLEY AND MUSHROOMS

½ cup chopped onion
4 tablespoons butter or
margarine
½ cup pearl barley
1 teaspoon salt

¼ teaspoon pepper
½ pound mushrooms,
sliced
2 cups chicken stock

1. Heat butter in skillet and sauté onion until barely soft. Add barley and brown lightly.
2. Combine all ingredients in cooker.
3. Cook on low 5 hours.

Yield: 4-5 servings

KASHA

"Kasha" is the Russian word for cooked, hulled grain —usually buckwheat. The English term is "buckwheat groats," which doesn't sound nearly so appetizing. Try kasha with a beef stew, or with roast poultry.

1 cup kasha	1 egg, lightly beaten
2 cups beef or chicken stock	1 teaspoon salt
	½ teaspoon pepper

1. In saucepan, heat stock to boiling.
2. In cooker, mix kasha and egg until kasha kernels are coated. Add boiling stock and seasonings.
3. Cook on high 1 hour.

Yield: 4 servings

Variation: After kasha is done, turn cooker to low and stir in the following: 1 cup sour cream, ¼ cup light cream, 1 tablespoon dill, and additional salt and pepper to taste. Heat through. This variation will yield about 6 servings.

GREEN RICE

This is a good accompaniment for almost any kind of meat stew. If you have fresh herbs on hand, use them instead of—or along with—the chopped parsley.

1 13-ounce can evaporated milk
½ cup cooking oil
2 eggs
1 medium onion, chopped
1 clove garlic, minced
1 cup parsley, chopped
3 cups cooked rice (1 cup raw)
2 cups cheese, grated (Cheddar, Swiss, or Muenster, or a combination)
salt and pepper to taste
1½ teaspoons salt
¼ teaspoon pepper

1. Combine milk, oil and eggs.
2. Add all other ingredients.
3. Place in well-greased cooker.
4. Cook on high 1 hour, then switch to low 4 hours. or cook on automatic for 3 hours.

Yield: 6 servings

Desserts

The best desserts for a slow cooker are fruits, which gain flavor as they simmer with spices, wine or fruit juice. They're good either warm or chilled, either plain or topped with cream, a sauce or ice cream. A slow cooker is also a simple way to make rich tea breads. Only a few recipes are included here. But you can try your hand at almost any baking-powder or soda bread (not a raised bread): apricot, cranberry, prune, or pumpkin are all possibilities. Note that if you use the dry method (as with apple cake or flowerpot banana bread), you should cover your container with paper towels. With the steam method (as with Boston brown bread), you add water to the pot and cover your container with aluminum foil. Depending on the size and shape of your cooker, you can try this type of bread in molds as well as the containers suggested here.

BAKED APPLES

5-6 medium apples,
    cored and peeled
    about 1 inch down
½ cup sugar

2 tablespoons raisins
1 teaspoon cinnamon
2 tablespoons butter
½ cup water

1. Mix sugar, raisins and cinnamon.
2. Stuff apples with sugar mixture and dot them with butter.
3. Pour water into cooker. Add apples.
4. Cook on low 7-8 hours.

Yield: 5-6 servings

Note: For a simpler version, try substituting maple syrup for the sugar and cinnamon.

APPLES AND PINEAPPLE

5-6 medium apples,
  peeled and cored
2 tablespoons dark
  brown sugar
1 teaspoon cinnamon

½ cup canned crushed
  pineapple, drained
  (reserve liquid)
pineapple juice
¼ cup chopped walnuts

1. Mix sugar, cinnamon and pineapple.
2. Stuff apples with sugar mixture.
3. If reserved pineapple liquid does not total ½ cup,
   add extra juice. Pour into cooker.
4. Add apples to cooker and sprinkle with walnuts.
5. Cook on low 7-8 hours.

Yield: 5-6 servings

APPLES A LA GREQUE

6 large apples, quartered, pared and cored
4 dried figs, minced
2 tablespoons raisins
2 tablespoons chopped walnuts
2 tablespoons blanched slivered almonds

½ teaspoon cinnamon
¼ cup sugar
¼ cup brandy (optional)
⅛ teaspoon nutmeg
½ cup orange juice or water

1. Combine all ingredients in cooker.
2. Cook on low 3-4 hours.

Yield: 6-8 servings

CINNAMON APPLES

Warm or chilled, these are a delicious accompaniment to roast pork or pork chops. They will be a nice rosy color if you use candy cinnamon drops. (If these aren't available, a drop or two of food coloring will do the trick.)

4-6 apples, pared and
   cored
 1 cup sugar
3-4 cloves

1 tablespoon red candy
   cinnamon drops (if
   not available, use
   1½ teaspoons cinna-
   mon)
1 cup water

1. Combine all ingredients in cooker.
2. Cook on low 6-8 hours, or on automatic 3-4 hours.

Yield: 4-6 servings

APPLESAUCE

It is difficult to write very precise directions for apple-sauce, since the type of apples used makes quite a difference, as does their age (older ones require more moisture, for instance). Let your taste be your guide.

6-8 cooking apples, quartered, pared, cored and chopped	½ teaspoon vanilla or almond extract
⅔-1 cup sugar	¼ teaspoon nutmeg
1 teaspoon cinnamon	1 cup water

1. Combine all ingredients in cooker.
2. Cook on low 5-6 hours.

Yield: 6-8 servings

Note: You may want to chop the apples coarsely before cooking them, then mash them after they're cooked; it's easier that way.

STEWED APRICOTS

1 or more packages
  dried apricots

1. Place apricots in cooker. Cover with water.
2. Cook on low 3-4 hours.

Yield: 4-6 servings (1 package)

Variation: To make a dessert sauce for cake or ice cream, purée 1 cup cooked apricots in a blender or food mill. Then add the following: 1 cup sugar, pinch salt, ¾ cup sour cream and 1 tablespoon cognac (optional).

BAKED BANANAS

6 ripe bananas, peeled,
cut in half, and each
half split lengthwise
1½ tablespoons lemon
juice
3 tablespoons orange
marmalade

3 tablespoons sherry
or muscatel wine
3 tablespoons melted
butter or margarine
3 tablespoons brown
sugar

1. Place bananas in cooker, sprinkling with lemon
   juice and spreading thinly with marmalade.
2. Mix together wine, butter and sugar, and spoon
   over bananas.
3. Cook on low 2-3 hours.

Yield: 6 servings

PEACHES IN BOURBON

6-8 peaches, peeled   ½ cup water
6-8 whole cloves   ½ cup Bourbon whiskey
1½ cups brown sugar

1. Insert a clove into each of the peaches. Place in cooker.
2. Mix sugar, water and whiskey; pour over peaches.
3. Cook on high 3-4 hours, or on automatic 5 hours.

Yield: 6-8 servings

PEARS IN RED WINE

4-6 russet or bosc pears, peeled
8-12 whole cloves
1 cup firmly packed dark brown sugar
1 cup sweet red wine
1-2 pieces stick cinnamon (if not available, use 1 teaspoon powdered cinnamon)

1. Insert two cloves into each pear. Place in cooker.
2. Mix sugar and wine; pour over pears. Add cinnamon.
3. Cook on high 3-4 hours, or on automatic 5 hours.

Yield: 4-6 servings

SPICED PRUNES

A good dessert either hot or chilled. It also goes well as a side dish with pork or roast duck or goose.

1 pound dried prunes
2 tablespoons brown
 sugar
2 cups orange juice
¼ cup sweet red wine

1 piece lemon peel
1 tablespoon cinnamon
1 teaspoon ground
 cloves
1 teaspoon nutmeg

1. Place prunes in cooker.
2. Mix sugar, orange juice and wine; pour over prunes.
3. Add remaining ingredients to cooker.
4. Cook on high 4-6 hours, or on automatic 5 hours.

Yield: 8-10 servings

STEWED RHUBARB

1½ pounds rhubarb, cut into ½-inch slices	½ cup water ½-⅔ cup sugar pinch salt

1. Combine all ingredients in cooker.
2. Cook on low 4-5 hours.

Yield: 6 servings

Variations: Add 1 pint cleaned, halved strawberries about 30 minutes before removing rhubarb from cooker. Or try seasoning with ¼ teaspoon cinnamon or ginger.

RHUBARB AND ORANGE COMPOTE

2 oranges
1½ cups sugar
¼ teaspoon cinnamon
4 cups rhubarb,
 washed and cut into

1-inch pieces (about
 1¼ pounds)
2 tablespoons Cognac
 or Grand Marnier
 (optional)
2 oranges

1. Peel 2 oranges and cut the peelings into narrow julienne strips about an inch long. Simmer in water for 5 minutes. Drain and reserve.
2. Squeeze the oranges. Combine the juice in a saucepan with sugar and cinnamon; heat until sugar is dissolved.
3. Place rhubarb in cooker, sprinkling it with reserved orange strips. Pour orange syrup over it.
4. Cook on low 4-5 hours.
5. Place cooked rhubarb in serving dish. Stir in liqueur, if used. Garnish with 2 oranges peeled, sliced and cut in quarters. Chill at least 4 hours.

Yield: 6 servings

SWEET POTATO PUDDING

This satisfying dessert is somewhat like an extra-rich pumpkin pie (without the crust). If you make a company dinner in your slow cooker earlier in the day, you can remove it to a casserole and then make this, as it takes a relatively short time to prepare.

2½ cups mashed, cooked sweet potatoes or yams (about 1½ pounds)
¾ cup light brown sugar
1 tablespoon molasses
1 teaspoon cinnamon
1 teaspoon ginger

¼ teaspoon nutmeg
½ teaspoon salt
3 eggs, beaten
peel of ½ tangerine or orange, cut into thin julienne strips

Cointreau or Grand Marnier (optional)
heavy cream

1. In a bowl, combine all ingredients except liqueur and cream.
2. Place in well-greased cooker.
3. Cook on high 2-3 hours.
4. Remove from cooker and sprinkle with liqueur, if desired. Serve with cream.

Yield: 6 servings

RICE PUDDING

2½ cups cooked rice
1½ cups evaporated
  milk
⅔ cup brown sugar
3 tablespoons butter
  or margarine

3 eggs, beaten
1 teaspoon vanilla
½ teaspoon nutmeg
½ teaspoon cinnamon
½ cup raisins or
  chopped dates

1. Grease cooker well.
2. Combine all ingredients in cooker and mix thoroughly.
3. Cook on low 4-6 hours, or on automatic 3 hours.

Yield: 6 servings

APPLE CAKE

Be sure you have an empty 2-pound coffee can on hand before you start this recipe.

2 cups sugar
1 cup cooking oil
2 eggs
2 teaspoons vanilla
2 cups flour
1 teaspoon salt

1 teaspoon baking soda
1 teaspoon nutmeg
2 cups apples, unpeeled, chopped fine
1 cup raisins or nuts

1. Sift together flour, salt, soda and nutmeg.
2. In separate bowl, beat together sugar, oil, and eggs; add vanilla.
3. To sugar mixture, add chopped apples and stir well. Then add flour mixture and raisins or nuts, and mix.
4. Grease and flour a 2-pound coffee can.
5. Pour cake mixture into can and set can in cooker. Cover with 2-3 paper towels.
6. Cover and cook on high 3½ hours. Do not lift lid, even to peek, until last hour.

Yield: 1 large cake

FLOWERPOT BANANA BREAD

The container is unusual—and so is the shape of the bread—but you might like to try it for a change.

2 cups sifted flour
1 teaspoon baking soda
½ teaspoon salt
½ cup butter or margarine
1 cup sugar
2 eggs

1 cup mashed, quite ripe bananas (2-3 bananas)
⅓ cup milk
1 teaspoon lemon juice
½ cup chopped walnuts

1. Sift together flour, soda and salt.
2. In a separate bowl, cream butter, then add sugar, eggs and bananas, blending thoroughly.
3. Combine milk and lemon juice.
4. To banana mixture, add alternately flour and milk mixtures, then stir in nuts.
5. Use a new 6½-inch (top diameter) clay flowerpot. Prepare as follows, after washing: grease, line with wax paper, and grease again.
6. Pour cake mixture into flowerpot and set pot in cooker. Cover with 2-3 paper towels.
7. Cover and cook on high 4-5 hours. Do not lift lid, even to peek, until last hour.

Yield: 1 large "pot" of bread

BOSTON BROWN BREAD

Developed by early American colonists to accompany—you guessed it—Boston baked beans. Good too as a tea bread or for breakfast. Delicious heated and spread with cream cheese. (Note that this requires an empty 1-pound coffee can.)

⅓ cup sifted white flour	⅓ cup whole-wheat flour
⅓ teaspoon baking powder	⅓ cup chopped nuts
⅓ teaspoon baking soda	¼ cup molasses
⅓ teaspoon salt	⅔ cup buttermilk or sour milk
⅓ cup yellow cornmeal	⅓ cup raisins

1. Sift white flour with baking powder, soda and salt.
2. Stir in cornmeal and whole-wheat flour. Add remaining ingredients and beat well.
3. Grease and flour a 1-pound coffee can.
4. Pour 3 cups water in cooker, place can inside, and cover with sheet of aluminum foil that extends beyond cooker.
5. Cover and cook on high 4-5 hours.

Yield: 1 small loaf

Note: Recipe may be doubled for 2-pound coffee can or tripled for 3-pound can. For larger sizes, use only 2 cups water in cooker.

Index